KOREAN GRAMMAR CANVAS

WORKBOOK for BEGINNERS 1

Korean Grammar Canvas : WORKBOOK for Beginners ❶

Written by Miss Vicky (Hyojeong Shim)
Publisher Kyudo Chung
Published by Darakwon

First Published 2025. 10. 30

Editorial Planner Hyukju Kwon, Taekwang Kim
Editor-in Chief Huchun Lee
Editor Hyoeun Kim

Designed by SINGTA Design
Illustrated by Gentle mellow (www.instagram.com/gentlemellow/)
Proofread by Anthony Kourakis

DARAKWON

Darakwon Bldg., 211 Munbal–ro, Paju–si, Gyeonggi–do, Republic of Korea 10881
Tel : 02–736–2031
Fax : 02–732–2037
(Marketing Dept. ext.: 250~252, Editorial Dept. ext.: 291~296)

ISBN 978-89-277-7545-4 13710

http://www.darakwon.co.kr
http://www.darakwonusa.com

Visit the Darakwon homepage to learn about our other publications and promotions and to download the contents in MP3 format.

KOREAN GRAMMAR CANVAS

Written by **Miss Vicky**

초급 한국어 문법 **워크북**

WORKBOOK for BEGINNERS

1

DARAKWON

The Author's Message

Welcome to this workbook, everyone!

I began writing the beginner Korean grammar series in July 2024, and now, a little over a year later, it has grown into four volumes: two main books and two workbooks.

Through the process of working on these books, I learned a valuable lesson: when you work alongside people who share the same purpose and heart, the results become even more meaningful.

This workbook was refined through my small group classes, where I taught nine students using the main volumes *Korean Grammar Palette for Beginners* 1 and 2. By seeing firsthand which parts students struggled with, which exercises helped them most, and which areas needed further reinforcement, I was able to shape this workbook with more thoughtfulness and depth. I also added new types of exercises and explanations to better support learners where they might need additional guidance.

For that, I want to thank the nine students who joined me so diligently for two months. Without their active participation, thoughtful questions, and sincere feedback, this workbook might have turned out much thinner and less complete.

I would like also to express my heartfelt gratitude to the editors and publishing staff at Darakwon, who have always paid close attention to my books and worked hard to reflect my wishes. It was their idea to publish both the main book and the workbook, and I am grateful that, as a result, we are able to provide Korean language learners with such rich and comprehensive resources.

When writing this workbook, I hoped it could be the kind of book learners would find useful even when used on its own. Since many learners prefer solving problems to reading explanations, my wish was that this workbook alone would still allow them to grasp grammar concepts and sentence structures with ease through a variety of thoughtfully crafted exercises. At the same time, I believe this book works best as a companion: ideally, you would study *Korean Grammar Palette* 1 first, and then use this workbook to complement, strengthen, and expand on what you've learned.

Either way, I hope you enjoy working through this workbook, and that it may serve as solid ground for your limitless growth in Korean.

With joy, sincerity, and love,

Vicky

How to use this book

This book consists of two parts: Part 1, the Workbook, and Part 2, the Final Sentence-Building Practice.

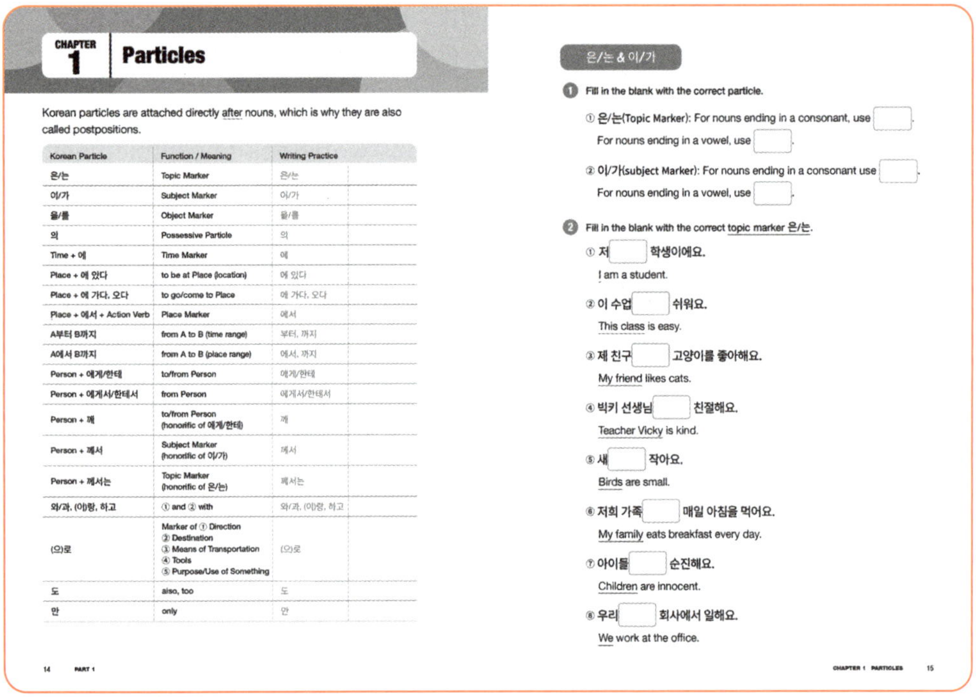

CHAPTER 1 Particles

Korean particles are attached directly after nouns, which is why they are also called postpositions.

Korean Particle	Function / Meaning	Writing Practice
은/는	Topic Marker	은/는
이/가	Subject Marker	이/가
을/를	Object Marker	을/를
의	Possessive Particle	의
Time + 에	Time Marker	에
Place + 에 있다	to be at Place (location)	에 있다
Place + 에 가다, 오다	to go/come to Place	에 가다, 오다
Place + 에서 + Action Verb	Place Marker	에서
A부터 B까지	from A to B (time range)	부터, 까지
A에서 B까지	from A to B (place range)	에서, 까지
Person + 에게/한테	to/from Person	에게/한테
Person + 에게서/한테서	from Person	에게서/한테서
Person + 께	to/from Person (honorific of 에게/한테)	께
Person + 께서	Subject Marker (honorific of 이/가)	께서
Person + 께서는	Topic Marker (honorific of 은/는)	께서는
와/과, (이)랑, 하고	① and ② with	와/과, (이)랑, 하고
(으)로	Marker of ① Direction ② Destination ③ Means of Transportation ④ Tools ⑤ Purpose/Use of Something	(으)로
도	also, too	도
만	only	만

14 PART 1

은/는 & 이/가

1. Fill in the blank with the correct particle.
   - ① 은/는(Topic Marker): For nouns ending in a consonant, use ____.
     For nouns ending in a vowel, use ____.
   - ② 이/가(subject Marker): For nouns ending in a consonant use ____.
     For nouns ending in a vowel, use ____.

2. Fill in the blank with the correct topic marker 은/는.
   - ① 저 ____ 학생이에요.
     I am a student.
   - ② 이 수업 ____ 쉬워요.
     This class is easy.
   - ③ 제 친구 ____ 고양이를 좋아해요.
     My friend likes cats.
   - ④ 빅키 선생님 ____ 친절해요.
     Teacher Vicky is kind.
   - ⑤ 새 ____ 작아요.
     Birds are small.
   - ⑥ 저희 가족 ____ 매일 아침을 먹어요.
     My family eats breakfast every day.
   - ⑦ 아이들 ____ 순진해요.
     Children are innocent.
   - ⑧ 우리 ____ 회사에서 일해요.
     We work at the office.

CHAPTER 1 PARTICLES 15

Part 1: Workbook

Grammar Tables

At the beginning of each chapter, you'll find a table that summarizes all the key expressions introduced in the main book. You can use these tables to review each topic at a glance, and you may also copy them out by hand in the space provided.

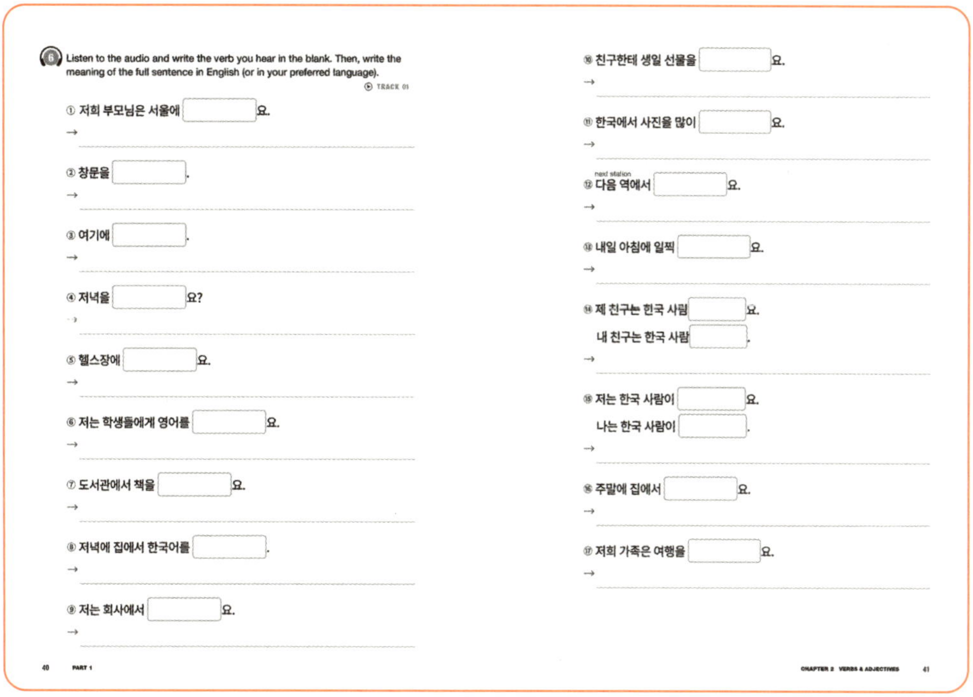
Listen to the audio and write the verb you hear in the blank. Then, write the meaning of the full sentence in English (or in your preferred language).

TRACK 01

① 저희 부모님은 서울에 [ ]요.
→

② 창문을 [ ].
→

③ 여기에 [ ].
→

④ 저녁을 [ ]요?
→

⑤ 헬스장에 [ ]요.
→

⑥ 저는 학생들에게 영어를 [ ]요.
→

⑦ 도서관에서 책을 [ ]요.
→

⑧ 저녁에 집에서 한국어를 [ ].
→

⑨ 저는 회사에서 [ ]요.
→

⑩ 친구한테 생일 선물을 [ ]요.
→

⑪ 한국에서 사진을 많이 [ ]요.
→

⑫ 다음 역에서 (next station) [ ]요.
→

⑬ 내일 아침에 일찍 [ ]요.
→

⑭ 제 친구는 한국 사람 [ ]요.
내 친구는 한국 사람 [ ].
→

⑮ 저는 한국 사람이 [ ]요.
나는 한국 사람이 [ ].
→

⑯ 주말에 집에서 [ ]요.
→

⑰ 저희 가족은 여행을 [ ]요.
→

40 PART 1

CHAPTER 2 VERBS & ADJECTIVES 41

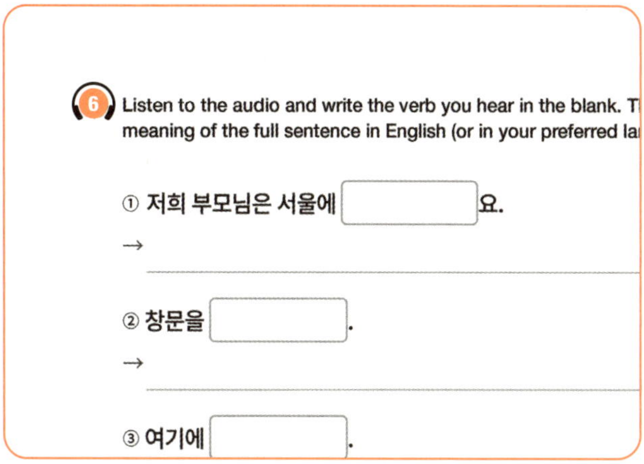
Listen to the audio and write the verb you hear in the blank. T
meaning of the full sentence in English (or in your preferred la

① 저희 부모님은 서울에 [ ]요.
→

② 창문을 [ ].
→

③ 여기에 [ ].

Audio Files
(www.darakwonusa.com)

Exercises

The workbook includes a variety of practice activities, such as fill-in-the-blank, dictation, translations, and more. Simply follow the instructions given for each exercise. For listening tasks, use the audio recordings accessible through the QR code.
(If you have the publisher's official edition of the book, the same QR code is also printed on the inside front cover of the book.)

⑥ 한국 사람들[ ] 매운 음식[ ] 좋아해요.
Korean people like spicy food.

⑦ 이 책[ ] 읽었어요.
I read this book.

⑧ 이 책[ ] 재미있어요.
This book is interesting.

Little Checkpoint Read & Tick ☑

1 An object is a grammatical term that refers to someone or something that an action is done to – in other words, the target of the action. For example, in the sentence "I know Jisu," Jisu is the object (the target) of the verb "know" – Jisu is someone who is known. In the sentence "I bought a bag," a bag is the object of the verb "buy" – it's what was bought. ☐

2 Only transitive verbs can take an object. Intransitive verbs do not need an object. ☐

3 Many learners get confused about whether the noun they're referring to in a sentence is the **subject** or the **object**. The easiest way to tell is to ask:

- Is an action being done to this noun? Is it the target of that action? → Then it's an **object**.
- Or are you simply describing something about it — such as its traits, tendencies, or actions it performs? → Then it's a **subject**. ☐

20 PART 1

의

❶ Fill in the blank with the correct particle.

① 이건 엄마[ ] 가방이에요.
This is Mom's bag.

② 저 사람은 우리[ ] 친구예요.
That person is our friend.

❷ What are two ways to say "my" in 존댓말?

① [ ] (full form)

② [ ] (contraction)

❸ What are two ways to say "my" in 반말?

① [ ] (full form)

② [ ] (contraction)

❹ What are two ways to say "your" in 반말?

① [ ] (full form)

② [ ] (contraction)

CHAPTER 1 PARTICLES 21

Checkpoints

There are little Checkpoint sections in between the exercises where the key points of each grammar pattern are neatly summarized for quick review. Once you've read and understood them, simply tick the box. If there's anything you don't understand, feel free to go back to the main book and read the explanation again.

Basic Korean Sentence Structure

Before we start, let's go over the essential rules of Korean word order and sentence structure.

1 **The basic word order is Subject-Object-Verb (SOV).**
The predicate — which can be a verb or an adjective — comes at the end of the sentence.

e.g. 저 - 한국어 - 배워요.
I Korean learn
not 저 - 배워요 - 한국어.
I learn Korean

2 **Korean particles** are placed after nouns.

3 **Adjectives** in Korean can function either as ① predicates or as ② modifiers that provide information about "what kind of noun." When used as modifiers, adjectives are placed directly before the noun.

Grammar Review Sections

In some chapters, you'll also find a section at the beginning that reviews the basic grammar patterns. Be sure to look over this part before starting the exercises.

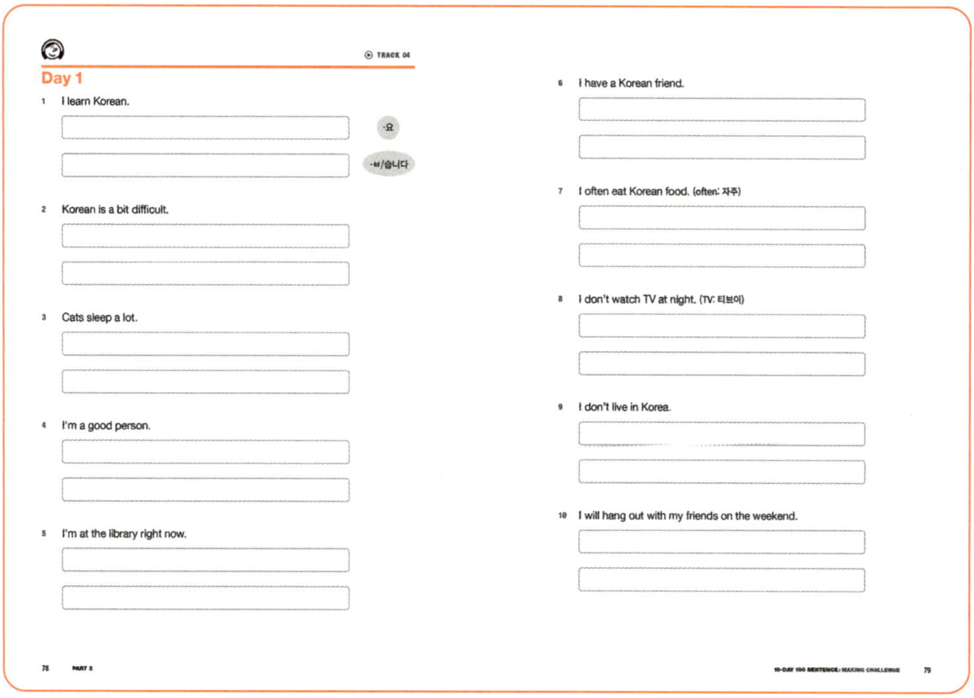

TRACK 04

Day 1

1 I learn Korean.

-요

-ㅂ/습니다

2 Korean is a bit difficult.

3 Cats sleep a lot.

4 I'm a good person.

5 I'm at the library right now.

6 I have a Korean friend.

7 I often eat Korean food. (often: 자주)

8 I don't watch TV at night. (TV: 티브이)

9 I don't live in Korea.

10 I will hang out with my friends on the weekend.

78 PART 2

10-DAY 100 SENTENCE: MAKING CHALLENGE 79

Day 10

91 I speak English and Korean.

92 Mom didn't call me today.

Part 2: 100-Sentence Challenge

This section offers daily practice where you create 10 sentences each day. After writing your sentences, check the answers provided. You can also use the audio files to check pronunciation and rhythm, or to practice dictation.

Answer Key

After completing the exercises, check your answers.

Vocabulary QR Codes

In this section, you will find two QR codes. The first QR code allows you to download a PDF file containing 200 Korean nouns and adverbs from this book. The other QR code takes you to Quizlet, where you can study the verbs, adjectives, nouns, and adverbs included in this book.

Table of Contents

CHAPTER 2 VERBS & ADJECTIVES

PART 1

Workbook

Basic Korean Sentence Structure

Before we start, let's go over the essential rules of Korean word order and sentence structure.

1 **The basic word order is Subject–Object–Verb (SOV).**
The predicate — which can be a verb or an adjective — comes at the end of the sentence.

e.g. 저 - 한국어 - 배워요.
I Korean learn

not 저 - 배워요 - 한국어.
I learn Korean

2 **Korean particles** are placed after nouns.

3 **Adjectives** in Korean can function either as ① predicates or as ② modifiers that provide information about "what kind of noun." When used as modifiers, adjectives are placed directly before the noun.

4 **Adverbs** can be placed anywhere before verbs. If an adverb gives direct information about the verb, it is usually placed immediately before it.

5 **Adverbial phrases** that express time and place usually appear toward the beginning of the sentence, right after the subject (or topic).

6 **Sentence endings** are the very last element in a sentence, and they are attached to the predicate (either the verb or adjective that the sentence ends with).

7 To tell whether a sentence is in 존댓말 or 반말, you can look for fixed words like 저 or 나, but more commonly, it's determined by whether sentence endings like -요 or -ㅂ/습니다 are used.

CHAPTER 1 Particles

Korean particles are attached directly after nouns, which is why they are also called postpositions.

Korean Particle	Function / Meaning	Writing Practice	
은/는	Topic Marker	은/는	
이/가	Subject Marker	이/가	
을/를	Object Marker	을/를	
의	Possessive Particle	의	
Time + 에	Time Marker	에	
Place + 에 있다	to be at Place (location)	에 있다	
Place + 에 가다, 오다	to go/come to Place	에 가다, 오다	
Place + 에서 + Action Verb	Place Marker	에서	
A부터 B까지	from A to B (time range)	부터, 까지	
A에서 B까지	from A to B (place range)	에서, 까지	
Person + 에게/한테	to/from Person	에게/한테	
Person + 에게서/한테서	from Person	에게서/한테서	
Person + 께	to/from Person (honorific of 에게/한테)	께	
Person + 께서	Subject Marker (honorific of 이/가)	께서	
Person + 께서는	Topic Marker (honorific of 은/는)	께서는	
와/과, (이)랑, 하고	① and ② with	와/과, (이)랑, 하고	
(으)로	Marker of ① Direction ② Destination ③ Means of Transportation ④ Tools ⑤ Purpose/Use of Something	(으)로	
도	also, too	도	
만	only	만	

은/는 & 이/가

1 Fill in the blank with the correct particle.

① 은/는(Topic Marker): For nouns ending in a consonant, use [ ].
For nouns ending in a vowel, use [ ].

② 이/가(Subject Marker): For nouns ending in a consonant use [ ]. For nouns ending in a vowel, use [ ].

2 Fill in the blank with the correct topic marker 은/는.

① 저 [ ] 학생이에요.
I am a student.

② 이 수업 [ ] 쉬워요.
This class is easy.

③ 제 친구 [ ] 고양이를 좋아해요.
My friend likes cats.

④ 빅키 선생님 [ ] 친절해요.
Teacher Vicky is kind.

⑤ 새 [ ] 작아요.
Birds are small.

⑥ 저희 가족 [ ] 매일 아침을 먹어요.
My family eats breakfast every day.

⑦ 아이들 [ ] 순진해요.
Children are innocent.

⑧ 우리 [ ] 회사에서 일해요.
We work at the office.

3 Fill in the blank with the correct topic marker 이/가.

① 이 수업 [ ] 쉬워요.

This class is easy.

② 제 친구 [ ] 고양이를 좋아해요.

My friend likes cats.

③ 빅키 선생님 [ ] 친절해요.

Teacher Vicky is kind.

④ 새 [ ] 작아요.

The bird is small.

⑤ 저희 가족 [ ] 매일 아침을 먹어요.

My family eats breakfast every day.

⑥ 아이들 [ ] 순진해요.

Children are innocent.

⑦ 우리 [ ] 주말에 일해요.

We work on the weekends.

4 Write the contracted form when the following nouns are combined with the topic marker 은/는.

① 저는 여자예요. I'm a woman.

→ [ ]

② 너는 내 친구야. You are my friend.

→ [ ]

③ 이거는 맛있어요. This is delicious.

→ [ ]

5 Write the correct final form when the following nouns are combined with the subject marker 이/가.

① 저 + 가 했어요. I did it.

→ [ ]

② 이거 + 가 제 차예요. This is my car.

→ [ ]

③ 너 + 가 맞아. You are right.

→ [ ]

Little Checkpoint Read & Tick ☑

1 **Topic** vs. **Subject**: The **topic** is what the sentence is mainly about — the overall focus — while the **subject** is the one doing the action or being described. ☐

2. In many cases, the topic and subject can be the same. For example, in **저는 한국어를 배워요** (I learn Korean), **저** (I) is both the **topic** of the sentence (the sentence is about me) and the **subject** of the verb **배우다** (to learn). ☐

3. However, this is not always the case. Something can be the **subject** of a verb (or adjective) without being the main **topic**, and vice versa — something can be the main **topic** without being the **subject**. ☐

4 **은/는** and **이/가** also have many other uses and are used in different contexts and situations to add different nuance and emphasis. For example, **지수는 학생이에요** and **지수가 학생이에요** both mean

"Jisu is a student", but they would be used in different contexts and convey different nuances. ☐

5 For the various differences between 은/는 and 이/가, please refer to the main book. However, as a beginner, it is not necessary to fully understand all of these differences. For now, you can think of 은/는 as highlighting the main topic or providing general information about something, while 이/가 specifies or clarifies a particular detail, often focusing on what is new, specific, or emphasized. ☐

6 It's also fine to omit 은/는 or 이/가 in your sentence and just use the noun. In fact, you can even omit the topic or subject entirely if it's clear from context what you're talking about.
(e.g., **저는 한국어를 배워요. 한국 문화를 좋아해요.** I learn Korean. I like Korean culture. — In both sentences, the topic/subject ("I") is obvious from context, so it is omitted in the second sentence.) ☐

을/를

1 Fill in the blank with the correct particle.

을/를(Object Marker) : For nouns ending in a consonant, use ______. For nouns ending in a vowel, use ______.

2 Fill in the blank with the correct object marker 을/를.

① 저는 가방 ______ 샀어요.

I bought a bag.

② 제 친구는 한국 음식 ______ 좋아해요.

My friend likes Korean food.

③ 우리는 한국어 ______ 배워요.

We learn Korean.

④ 그 사람 [ ] 알아요.

I know that person.

⑤ 어제 친구 [ ] 만났어요.

I met a friend yesterday.

⑥ 영화 [ ] 봤어요.

I watched a movie.

⑦ 시장에서 엄마 [ ] 봤어요.

I saw Mom at the market.

⑧ 물 [ ] 좀 마셔요.

Drink some water.

3 **Fill in the blank with either the subject marker 이/가 or the object marker 을/를.**

(This question tests whether the noun you're trying to express is the **subject** or the **object** of the sentence — a point many students often get confused about.)

① 아빠 [ ] 컴퓨터 [ ] 고쳤어요.

Dad fixed the computer.

② 컴퓨터 [ ] 비싸요.

The computer is expensive.

③ 친구 [ ] 사진 [ ] 올렸어요.

My friend posted a photo.

④ 이 사진 [ ] 너무 예뻐요.

This picture is so beautiful.

⑤ 저는 한국 사람들 [ ] 좋아해요.

I like Korean people.

⑥ 한국 사람들 [ ] 매운 음식 [ ] 좋아해요.

Korean people like spicy food.

⑦ 이 책 [ ] 읽었어요.

I read this book.

⑧ 이 책 [ ] 재미있어요.

This book is interesting.

Little Checkpoint Read & Tick ☑

1 An object is a grammatical term that refers to someone or something that an action is done to — in other words, the target of the action. For example, in the sentence "I know Jisu," Jisu is the object (the target) of the verb "know" — Jisu is someone who is known. In the sentence "I bought a bag," a bag is the object of the verb "buy" — it's what was bought. ☐

2 Only transitive verbs can take an object. Intransitive verbs do not need an object. ☐

3 Many learners get confused about whether the noun they're referring to in a sentence is the **subject** or the **object**. The easiest way to tell is to ask:

- Is an action being done to this noun? Is it the target of that action? → Then it's an **object**.
- Or are you simply describing something about it — such as its traits, tendencies, or actions it performs? → Then it's a **subject**. ☐

의

1 Fill in the blank with the correct particle.

① 이건 엄마 [ ] 가방이에요.

This is Mom's bag.

② 저 사람은 우리 [ ] 친구예요.

That person is our friend.

2 What are two ways to say "my" in 존댓말?

① [ ] (full form)

② [ ] (contraction)

3 What are two ways to say "my" in 반말?

① [ ] (full form)

② [ ] (contraction)

4 What are two ways to say "your" in 반말?

① [ ] (full form)

② [ ] (contraction)

에 & 에서

1 Fill in the blank with 에, 에서 or leave it blank.

① 일요일 ______ 쉴 거예요.
I will take a rest on Sunday.

② 월요일 ______ 만나자.
Let's meet on Monday.

③ 회사 ______ 있어요.
I'm at the office.

④ 차가 주차장 ______ 있어요.
The car is at the parking lot.

⑤ 회사 ______ 일해요.
I work at the office.

⑥ 제 친구는 한국 ______ 살아요.
My friend lives in Korea.

⑦ 카페 ______ 친구를 만났어요.
I met a friend at the coffee shop.

⑧ 어제 ______ 서울 ______ 갔어요.
I went to Seoul yesterday.

⑨ 우리 집 ______ 오세요.
Please come to my house.

⑩ 주말 ______ 도서관 ______ 책을 읽을 거예요.
I will read a book in the library on the weekend.

부터, 에서 & 까지

1 Fill in the blank with 부터, 에서 or 까지.

① 9월 ______ 12월 ______ 한국 대학교에서 공부해요.
I study at a Korean university from September to December.

② 여기 ______ 지하철역 ______ 얼마나 걸려요?
How long does it take from here to the subway station?

③ 내일 ______ 끝낼 거예요.
I will finish it by tomorrow.

④ 끝 ______ 포기하지 않을 거예요.
I won't give up until the end.

⑤ 커피 ______ 마셔요.
Let's drink coffee first.

⑥ 작년 ______ 한국에 있었어요.
I've been in Korea since last year.

⑦ 3월 ______ 한국에 있을 거예요.
I will stay in Korea till March.

에게(서)/한테(서)

1 Select the correct particle(s) in the parentheses, and then write the translation of each sentence.

Note: "Particle(s)" means that multiple correct answers may be possible.

① 친구(에게 / 한테 / 를) 말했어요.

→ ______

② 엄마(에게 / 한테 / 를) 전화할 거예요.

→ ______

③ 여자친구(에게 / 한테 / 를) 선물(에게 / 한테 / 을) 줄 거예요.

→ ______

④ 동료(에게 / 한테 / 를) 메일(에게 / 한테 / 을) 보냈어요.

→ ______

2 Select the correct particle(s) in the parentheses, and then write the translation of each sentence.

native teacher
① 원어민 선생님(에게 / 에게서 / 을) 한국어(한테 / 한테서 / 를) 배웠어요.

→ ______

apology
② 친구(한테 / 한테서 / 를) 사과(한테 / 한테서 / 를) 받았어요.

→ ______

news
③ 엄마(한테 / 한테서 / 를) 좋은 소식(한테 / 한테서 / 을) 들었어요.

→ ______

④ 여동생(에게 / 에게서 / 을) 책(한테 / 한테서 / 을) 빌렸어요.

→ ______

⑤ 빅키 선생님은 외국인들(에게 / 을) 한국어(에게 / 를) 가르쳐요.

→ ______

⑥ 저는 아이들(한테 / 을) 가르쳐요.

→ ______

⑦ 꽃(에 / 에게) 물을 줬어요?

→ ______

께 vs. 께서

1 Select the correct particle in the parentheses.

① 교수님(께 / 께서) 물어봤어요.
I asked the professor.

② 교수님(께 / 께서) 저한테 이 책을 주셨어요.
The professor gave me this book.

③ 빅키 선생님(께 / 께서) 한국어를 배웠어요.
I learned Korean from Teacher Vicky.

④ 빅키 선생님(께 / 께서) 이 책을 쓰셨어요.
Teacher Vicky wrote this book.

Little Checkpoint Read & Tick ☑

1 The particles **에게** & **한테** mean either "to [person]" or "from [person]," depending on the verb that follows. They are used only with nouns referring to people (or animals you wish to personify). ☐

2 **에게** and **한테** are always interchangeable. The only small difference is that **한테** sounds less formal than **에게**. ☐

3 When **에게/한테** means "from," you can also add **서** and say **에게서** or **한테서**. (This doesn't work when **에게/한테** means "to.") ☐

4 **께** is the honorific form of **에게/한테**, and it can also mean "to" or "from". However, **께서** (which has **서** attached to **께**) does not mean "from" like **에게서/한테서**. In fact, **께서** is the honorific form of the subject marker **이/가**; it's a different particle that has a completely different grammatical function. ☐

5 **에게/한테** is not used with non-human nouns like animals, plants, or insects (unless you intentionally want to personify them.) In such cases, **에** is used instead of **에게/한테**. (e.g., **나무에 물을 줬어요**, **벌레에 물렸어요**) ☐

와/과, (이)랑 & 하고

1 **Choose the meaning of the underlined particle based on the context, and then write the translation of each sentence.**

① 엄마<u>하고</u> 백화점에 갔어요. (and / with)

→ ______________________________

② 딸기<u>랑</u> 키위를 샀어요. (and / with)

→ ______________________________

③ 저는 딸이랑 아들이 있어요. (and / with)

→ ______________________________

④ 저는 봄과 겨울을 제일 좋아해요. (and / with)

→ ______________________________

⑤ 친구와 놀았어요. (and / with)

→ ______________________________

⑥ 저는 오늘 아빠하고 할머니랑 시장에 갔어요.
(and / with) (and / with)

→ ______________________________

2 Select one sentence where the particle is incorrectly written, and rewrite the phrase with the correct particle.

① 강아지랑 고양이를 키워요.

② 가게에서 펜하고 연필을 샀어요.

③ 아이들랑 저녁을 먹었어요.

④ 가족들과 여행을 갔어요.

⑤ 저와 함께 한국어를 배워요.

(으)로

1 Write the correct form of (으)로 to complete each sentence in the blank, and then translate the sentence into English (or your preferred language).

① 아침[ ] 빵과 커피를 먹었어요.

→ ______

② 오른쪽[ ] 가요.

→ ______

③ 선생님하고 한국어[ ] 얘기했어요.

→ ______

④ 서울역에서 일산까지 지하철[ ] 갔어요.

→ ______

⑤ 빨대(straw)[ ] 콜라(coke)를 마셨어요.

→ ______

⑥ 뭐[ ] 고를 거예요?

→ ______

도 & 만

1 Fill in each blank with the most natural particle (도 or 만) according to the context.

ⓐ 도　　　　ⓑ 만

① 저는 책을 좋아합니다. 영화 ________ 좋아합니다.

② 현금이(cash) 없습니다. 카드 ________ 있습니다.

③ 저는 의사입니다. 남편 ________ 의사입니다.

④ 친구들은 한국어를 못합니다. 저 ________ 잘합니다.

2 Which combination of particles best fits the blank in the sentence?

① 저는 도서관 ________ 공부합니다.

ⓐ 만에　ⓑ 만에서　ⓒ 에만　ⓓ 에서만

② 이 가게는 서울 ________ 있습니다.

ⓐ 만에　ⓑ 만에서　ⓒ 에만　ⓓ 에서만

③ 이번 여름에 한국에 갈 겁니다. 일본 ________ 갈 겁니다.

ⓐ 에도　ⓑ 에서도　ⓒ 도에　ⓓ 도에서

④ 저는 요즘 한국어 ________ 얘기합니다. (TWO correct answers)

ⓐ 로만　ⓑ 만으로　ⓒ 에만　ⓓ 만에

⑤ 한국어를 책으로 공부했습니다. 동영상 ________ 공부했습니다.

ⓐ 도으로 ⓑ 으로도

⑥ 제 비밀을 민지 ________ 말했습니다. (TWO correct answers)

ⓐ 한테만 ⓑ 만한테 ⓒ 에게만 ⓓ 만에게

⑦ 수진 씨 ________ 사진을 찍었습니다.

ⓐ 만하고 ⓑ 하고만

3 The following sentences have the particle written incorrectly. Write the correct version.

① 저는 한국어를 잘해요. 영어를도 잘해요.

→ [ ]

② 지수는 제 친구예요. 지호도가 제 친구예요.

→ [ ]

③ 저는 과일을 싫어해요. 파인애플을만 좋아해요.

→ [ ]

Little Checkpoint Read & Tick ☑

1 **하고**, (**이**)**랑**, **와**/**과** can mean either "and" or "with," depending on the context. It can be used with any noun when it means "and," but when it means "with," it should only be used with people. ☐

2 If the noun ends in a vowel, use **랑** or **와**; if it ends in a consonant, use **이랑** or **과**. **하고** does not change form regardless of whether the noun ends in a vowel or a consonant. ☐

3 With (**으**)**로**, use **로** after a noun ending in a vowel, and **으로** after a noun ending in a consonant. However, if the noun ends in **ㄹ**, you must still use **로**, even though **ㄹ** is a consonant. ☐

4 (**으**)**로** has various uses, but the most common ones include indicating direction, destination, means of transportation, tools, and marking a choice. ☐

5 When combined with other particles, **도** and **만** are usually placed last in the combination. An exception is when **만** is combined with (**으**)**로** – both **만으로** and **으로만** are acceptable. ☐

6 The particle **도** cannot be paired with topic, subject, or object markers (**은**/**는**, **이**/**가**, **을**/**를**). In contrast, **만** can combine with them (e.g., **나만이**, **그 사람만은**), often adding an extra nuance of emphasis or contrast. However, in everyday usage, both **도** and **만** are generally not used together with **은**/**는**, **이**/**가**, **을**/**를**, so you will most often see them attached directly after the noun or phrase without those markers. ☐

CHAPTER 2

Verbs & Adjectives

Basics of Korean Verbs

Let's go over the essentials of how Korean verbs work.

1 All Korean verbs have a base form (also called a dictionary form), such as 살다, 가다, 먹다, or 마시다.
All base forms end with -다.

2 The syllables before -다 in a base form are called the stem.

e.g. 살다's stem: 살
가다's stem: 가
먹다's stem: 먹
마시다's stem: 마시

3 The base form cannot be used as-is in a sentence. It must be conjugated (or combined with a certain ending or suffix) to be used in actual sentences.

4 How a verb is conjugated depends on its stem. Many verbs follow regular conjugation rules, but some verbs follow irregular rules. (Book 1 introduces only some irregular rules, while Book 2 covers them in more detail.)

1 Verbs

Regular Conjugation Rules

1 Fill in the blank with the correct Korean letter, syllable, or English word.

(1) Present Tense

When Stem ends with a final consonant

Rule 1 If the last character/syllable of the verb stem ends with a final consonant and they have either ㅏ or ㅗ in the vowel (e.g., 알다, 닫다, 놀다), they're conjugated by adding [______] (one syllable) after the stem.

Rule 2 If the last character/syllable of the verb stem ends with a final consonant and the vowel is anything other than ㅏ or ㅗ (e.g., 먹다, 읽다, 웃다, 만들다), they're conjugated by adding [______] (one syllable) after the stem.

When Stem ends with a vowel

Rule 3 If a verb stem ends in the vowel ㅏ, ㅓ, ㅕ, or ㅐ (e.g., 가다, 서다, 켜다, 보내다), you simply use the [______] (English word) itself to conjugate the verb.

Rule 4 If a verb stem ends in the vowel ㅗ (e.g., 오다, 보다), they're conjugated by replacing ㅗ with the vowel [______].

Rule 5 If a verb stem ends in the vowel ㅜ (e.g., 배우다, 주다), they're conjugated by replacing ㅜ with the vowel [______].

Rule 6 If a verb stem ends in the vowel ㅣ (e.g., 마시다, 가르치다), they're conjugated by replacing ㅣ with the vowel [______].

Rule 7 All verbs that end with -하다 (e.g., 공부하다, 일하다, 좋아하다) are conjugated as -[______] (one syllable).

(2) Past Tense

For past tense conjugation, simply add ☐ (final consonant) ☐ (one syllable) to the present tense form.

(3) Future Tense

Stem (that ends with a vowel) + ☐ (final consonant) + 거야 (반말) / 거예요 (존댓말)

Stem (that ends with a consonant) + ☐ (one syllable) + 거야/거예요

Little Checkpoint **Read & Tick** ☑

A Quick Look-Back at Some Irregular Verbs

1 듣다 (to listen) → 들어(요), 들었어(요), 들을 거야 / 들을 거예요

2 쓰다 (to write, to use) → 써(요), 썼어(요), 쓸 거야 / 쓸 거예요

3 **The ㄹ Irregular in Future Tense Conjugation**: When a verb stem ends in ㄹ, you don't need to add the extra suffix -을. Simply use the stem as it is and attach 거예요. (Since the stem already ends in ㄹ, there's no need to add another syllable that ends with ㄹ.)

e.g. 살다 → 살 거예요 (√), 살을 거예요 (×) ☐

2 **Which of the following can be expressed using the present tense form of Korean verbs? Check all that apply.**

☐ A. An action someone is currently doing

☐ B. Someone's usual habit or tendency

☐ C. A "Let's" statement (suggestion)

☐ D. An imperative sentence (command)

☐ E. Future plans (only when a specific future time is mentioned)

3 Let's practice conjugating the following verbs in Korean using the table below.

동사 Verb	현재 시제 Present Tense	과거 시제 Past Tense	미래 시제 Future Tense
가다 to go			
가르치다 to teach			
공부하다 to study			
기다리다 to wait			
끝내다 to finish			
넣다 to put (sth) in			
놀다 to play			
놓다 to put (sth) on top of something			
내리다 to get off			
닫다 to close			
도착하다 to arrive			
되다 to become			
듣다 to listen			
마시다 to drink			
만나다 to meet			
만들다 to make			
말하다 to talk, speak			
먹다 to eat			
물어보다 to ask			
받다 to receive			
배우다 to learn			
벗다 to take (clothing) off			

동사 Verb	현재 시제 Present Tense	과거 시제 Past Tense	미래 시제 Future Tense
보내다 ① to send ② to spend (time)			
보다 to see, to watch			
빌리다 to borrow			
사다 to buy			
사랑하다 to love			
살다 to live			
생각하다 to think			
서다 to stand			
쉬다 to rest			
시작하다 to start			
신다 to wear (shoes)			
싫어하다 to dislike, to hate			
싸우다 to fight			
쓰다 ① to use ② to write			
씻다 to wash			
앉다 to sit			
알다 to know			
없다 ① to not be (somewhere) ② to not have			
열다 to open			
오다 to come			
외우다 to memorize			
요리하다 to cook			
운동하다 to exercise			

동사 Verb	현재 시제 Present Tense	과거 시제 Past Tense	미래 시제 Future Tense
운전하다 to drive			
울다 to cry			
웃다 to laugh			
이야기하다 to talk			
일어나다 ① to get up ② to happen			
일하다 to work			
읽다 to read			
입다 to wear			
있다 ① to be (somewhere) ② to have			
자다 to sleep			
잘하다 to be good at (sth)			
전화하다 to call			
좋아하다 to like			
주다 to give			
지내다 to stay, to live			
(사진을) 찍다 to take photos			
청소하다 to clean			
출발하다 to depart			
춤을 추다 to dance			
켜다 to turn on			
키우다 to raise, to grow			
타다 to ride, to get in/on (a vehicle)			
하다 to do			

4 Fill in the table with the correct conjugations of 이다 and 아니다 in different contexts.

		존댓말	반말
Noun이다 (to be Noun)	When a noun ends in a vowel		
	When a noun ends in a consonant		
Noun이/가 아니다			

5 Fill in the blank using the correct conjugated form of the verb. Please use the -요 ending 존댓말.

① 이 단어를 [ ].

I know this word.

② 어제 친구를 [ ].

I met a friend yesterday.

③ 그 영화를 이미 [ ].

I watched that movie already.

④ 저는 항상 아침을 [ ].

I always eat breakfast.

⑤ 오늘 여기에서 [ ].

I will sleep here today.

⑥ 좀 [ ].

Rest a bit. (= Get some rest.)

⑦ 도서관에서 같이 [ ].

Let's study together at the library.

⑧ 사람들이 그냥 [ ]. 걱정 마세요!

People will just laugh. Don't worry!

⑨ A 이메일을 [ ]. I sent an email.

B [ ]. 고마워요. I received it. Thank you.

⑩ 아빠는 너무 열심히 [ ].

My dad works too hard.

⑪ 오늘 저희 가게에 손님들이 많이 [ ].

A lot of customers came to our store today.

⑫ 엄마는 아이들을 [ ].

My mom teaches children.

⑬ 지수 씨가 아마 [ ].

Jisu will probably know.

⑭ 물을 좀 [ ].

Drink some water.

⑮ 친구한테 [ ].

I gave it to my friend.

⑯ 한국 음식을 직접 [ ]. 가족들이 [ ].

I will make Korean food myself. My family will like it.

6 Listen to the audio and write the verb you hear in the blank. Then, write the meaning of the full sentence in English (or in your preferred language).

TRACK 01

① 저희 부모님은 서울에 [ ]요.

→ ______

② 창문을 [ ].

→ ______

③ 여기에 [ ].

→ ______

④ 저녁을 [ ]요?

→ ______

⑤ 헬스장에 [ ]요.

→ ______

⑥ 저는 학생들에게 영어를 [ ]요.

→ ______

⑦ 도서관에서 책을 [ ]요.

→ ______

⑧ 저녁에 집에서 한국어를 [ ].

→ ______

⑨ 저는 회사에서 [ ]요.

→ ______

⑩ 친구한테 생일 선물을 [   ]요.

→ ______________________________

⑪ 한국에서 사진을 많이 [   ]요.

→ ______________________________

next station
⑫ 다음 역에서 [   ]요.

→ ______________________________

⑬ 내일 아침에 일찍 [   ]요.

→ ______________________________

⑭ 제 친구는 한국 사람[   ]요.

내 친구는 한국 사람[   ].

→ ______________________________

⑮ 저는 한국 사람이 [   ]요.

나는 한국 사람이 [   ].

→ ______________________________

⑯ 주말에 집에서 [   ]요.

→ ______________________________

⑰ 저희 가족은 여행을 [   ]요.

→ ______________________________

7 Fill in the blank with either 이다, 이/가 있다 or 에 있다, by conjugating them in 존댓말.

① 이건 건물 [   ].

This is a building.

② 건물 [   ].

There is a building. / I have a building.

③ 건물 [   ].

I'm in a building.

④ 이 사람은 저희 언니 [   ].

This person is my sister.

⑤ 저는 언니 [   ].

I have a sister.

⑥ 언니가 집 [   ].

My sister is at home.

8 For each sentence in the above Question **7**, write a new sentence that has the opposite meaning in Korean.

① This is not a building.

= [   ]

② There is no building. / I don't have a building.

= [   ]

③ I'm not in a building.

= [   ]

④ This person is not my sister.

=

⑤ I don't have a sister.

=

⑥ My sister is not at home.

=

9 **Fill in the blank with the correct particle.**

① 동생 ___ 있어요. I have a younger sibling.

② 한국 ___ 친구 ___ 없어요. I don't have friends in Korea.

③ 작은 상자 ___ 있어요. There's a small box.

④ 가수 ___ 되고 싶어요. I want to be a singer.

⑤ 지수는 한국어 ___ 진짜 잘해요. Jisu is very good at Korean.

⑥ 저는 운동 ___ 못해요. I'm not good at sports.

⑦ 우리 집 ___ 와. Come to my house.

⑧ 내년 ___ 한국 ___ 갈 거예요. I will go to Korea next year.

Little Checkpoint Read & Tick ☑

Learners often get confused between **이다** and **있다**, and even within **있다**, it's a common mistake to mix up **이/가 있다** and **에 있다**.

Let's go over them again and highlight the key points.

❶ 이다 – Identification ☐

이다 is used when the subject is identified as a noun.
Structure: [Subject] + [Noun] + **이다**

e.g. **저는 학생이에요.** I am a student. (I = student)
이건 제 책이에요. This is my book. (This = my book)

Important Note: **이다** is not exactly the same as the English "to be." **이다** is only used with nouns, and never with adjectives. To express qualities or states (e.g., I am smart, This is big, That is tasty), adjectives should be used, not **이다**.

❷ 있다 – Existence / Possession / Location ☐

(1) 이/가 있다

① to exist / to be present; something exists in a place or situation
② to have; expanded meaning — if something exists in your life, it can also mean "to have."

e.g. **의자가 있어요.**
① There is a chair. ② I have a chair.
차가 있어요.
① There is a car. ② I have a car.

(2) 에 있다

This form is used to indicate that something or someone is **at a certain location**.

Structure: [Subject] + [Place] + **에 있다**

e.g. **저는 집에 있어요.** I'm at home.
책이 방에 있어요. The book is in my room.

2 Adjectives

Adjectives in Korean can be used in two main ways:

① **Conjugated and used as a predicate**

e.g. 고양이가 작아요. The cat is small.

날씨가 더워요. The weather is hot.

These sentences have both a subject and a predicate, making it a complete sentence.

② **Changed into a modifier form to describe a following noun**

e.g. 작은 고양이 small cat

더운 날씨 hot weather

These are not a complete sentence but a noun phrase. The word **작은** adds information about what kind of cat you are talking about, and the word **더운** adds information about what kind of weather you're talking about.

You can use these phrases to complete sentences like:

작은 고양이를 봤어요. I saw a small cat.

작은 고양이가 울어요. The small cat is crying.

Conjugation Rules

Adjectives follow the same conjugation rules as verbs, and the irregular rules are no exception.

While you'll find more focused and comprehensive questions on irregular patterns in Book 2, let's first take a look at two types of adjective irregulars that appear frequently:
those ending in ㅂ and those ending in ㅡ.

ㅂ-Irregular Conjugation

Many adjectives end in the consonant ㅂ, and these often follow the ㅂ irregular conjugation rule.

1 Fill in the blank with the correct syllable.

- Present Tense: Remove ㅂ from the stem and add [ ] (one syllable).
- Future Tense: Remove ㅂ from the stem and add [ ] (one syllable) 거야/거예요.

Little Checkpoint Read & Tick ☑

1 The ㅂ irregular rule applies not only to adjectives ending in ㅂ, but also to some verbs (although there are far more many adjectives that end in ㅂ than verbs.) ☐

2 However, there are a few exceptions — some words ending in ㅂ still follow the regular conjugation rule, such as 입다 (to wear) and 좁다 (to be narrow.) ☐

ㅡ -Irregular Conjugation

2 Fill in the blank with the correct vowel.

Present Tense

❶ If the stem has only one syllable, the vowel ㅡ is replaced with [______] (vowel) when conjugating.

❷ If the stem has more than one syllable, look at the syllable right before the one that contains ㅡ:

- If that syllable contains ㅏ or ㅗ, replace ㅡ with [______] (vowel).
- If it contains any other vowel, replace ㅡ with [______] (vowel).

3 Let's practice conjugating the following adjectives in Korean using the table below.

형용사 Adjective	현재 시제 Present Tense	과거 시제 Past Tense	미래 시제 Future Tense
가깝다 to be close			
가볍다 to be light			
간단하다 to be simple			
같다 / 똑같다 to be the same			
건강하다 to be healthy			
고맙다 to be thankful			
괜찮다 to be okay			
귀엽다 to be cute			
기쁘다 to be happy			
길다 to be long			
나쁘다 to be bad			
낮다 to be low			

형용사 Adjective	현재 시제 Present Tense	과거 시제 Past Tense	미래 시제 Future Tense
넓다 to be wide, to be spacious			
느리다 to be slow			
늦다 to be late			
달다 to be sweet			
덥다 to be hot			
두껍다 to be thick			
많다 to be many			
맛있다 to be delicious			
맛없다 to be not delicious			
멋지다 to be cool, to be amazing, to be handsome			
멀다 to be far			
무겁다 to be heavy			
무섭다 to be scary, to be scared			
미안하다 to be sorry			
바쁘다 to be busy			
반갑다 to be glad (to see someone)			
밝다 to be bright			
배고프다 to be hungry			
부드럽다 to be soft			
부지런하다 to be diligent			
불편하다 to be uncomfortable, to be inconvenient			

형용사 Adjective	현재 시제 Present Tense	과거 시제 Past Tense	미래 시제 Future Tense
비싸다 to be expensive			
시원하다 to be cool [weather]			
시끄럽다 to be noisy, to be loud			
싸다 to be cheap			
슬프다 to be sad			
쉽다 to be easy			
쓰다 to be bitter			
아름답다 to be beautiful			
아프다 to be sick			
어둡다 to be dark			
어렵다 to be difficult			
어리다 to be young			
예쁘다 to be pretty			
이상하다 to be strange			
외롭다 to be lonely			
유명하다 to be famous			
작다 to be small 키가 작다 to be short			
재미있다 to be fun, to be interesting			
재미없다 to be boring, to be bored			
조용하다 to be quiet			
좁다 to be narrow			
좋다 to be good			

형용사 Adjective	현재 시제 Present Tense	과거 시제 Past Tense	미래 시제 Future Tense
중요하다 to be important			
즐겁다 to be joyful			
짧다 to be short			
지루하다 to be boring, to be bored			
차갑다 to be cold [touch]			
착하다 to be nice, to be good-hearted			
춥다 to be cold [weather]			
친절하다 to be kind			
크다 to be big 키가 크다 to be tall			
편하다 to be comfortable, to be convenient			
피곤하다 to be tired			
행복하다 to be happy			
흐리다 ① to be blurry ② to be cloudy			
흔하다 to be common			
힘들다 to be challenging, to be difficult			

4 Fill in the blank with the adjective conjugated in the -요 ending.

① 오늘 날씨가 [ ]. 근데 조금 [ ].

The weather is good today. But it is a bit hot.

② 오늘 공기가 [ ]. 집에 있을 거예요.

The air is bad today. I will stay home.

③ 저 집이 진짜 [ ].

That house over there is really big.

④ 가방이 너무 [ ].

The bag is too small.

⑤ 지수 씨의 머리가 아주 [ ].

Jisu's hair is very long.

⑥ 커피가 너무 [ ].

The coffee is too sweet.

⑦ 선생님이 [ ].

The teacher is kind.

⑧ 호텔이 여기에서 너무 [ ]. 그래서 택시로 갈 거예요.

The hotel will be too far from here. So I'll go by taxi.

⑨ 저희 엄마는 요즘 너무 [ ].

My mom is too busy these days.

⑩ 시험이 조금 [ ].

The exam was a bit easy.

⑪ 얼음을 너무 많이 넣었어요. 너무 [ ].

I put in too much ice. It will be too cold.

⑫ 한국어는 [ ]. 근데 [ ].

Korean is difficult. But it's fun.

⑬ [ ]. 근데 조금 [ ].

It is delicious. But it is a bit spicy.

⑭ 기차는 너무 [ ]. 그냥 비행기로 가요.

Trains are too slow. Let's just go by plane.

⑮ 줄이 너무 [ ]. 배가 [ ].

The queue is too long. I am hungry.

5 Listen to the audio and complete the sentence by filling in the blank with the conjugated adjective you hear. Then, translate the whole sentence into English.

TRACK 02

① 이 신발이 정말 [ ]. 근데(but) 좀 [ ].

→

② 머리가 [ ].

→

③ 경치(view)가 정말 [ ].

→

④ 공항(airport)에 사람이 [ ].

→

⑤ 고양이가 [ ].

→

⑥ 도서관이 집에서 [ ].

→

⑦ 커피가 조금 [ ].

→

The Modifier Form of Adjectives

6 Fill in the blank with the correct letter and syllable.

Adjective's Modifier Form

Regular: Stem + [ ] / [ ]
final consonant one syllable

Irregular:

① The ㄹ ending adjectives: Remove ㄹ from the stem and add [ ].
final consonant

② The ㅂ ending adjectives: Remove ㅂ from the stem and add [ ].
one syllable

③ The -있다 and -없다 ending adjectives: Add [ ] instead of 은.
one syllable

7 Let's use this section to practice forming the modifier form of Korean adjectives.

Adjective (Base Form)	Modifier Form
가깝다	[ ] 공원 – a close/nearby park
가볍다	[ ] 점심 – a light lunch
간단하다	[ ] 문장 – a simple sentence
같다	[ ] 이름 – the same name
건강하다	[ ] 음식 – healthy food
고맙다	[ ] 친구 – a friend I feel thankful for
귀엽다	[ ] 아기 – a cute baby
기쁘다	[ ] 마음 – a happy heart
길다	[ ] 머리 – long hair
나쁘다	[ ] 사람 – a bad person
낮다	[ ] 건물 – a low building
넓다	[ ] 방 – a spacious room
느리다	[ ] 거북이 – a slow turtle
늦다	[ ] 시간 – a late time
달다	[ ] 도넛 – a sweet doughnut
덥다	[ ] 날씨 – hot weather
두껍다	[ ] 책 – a thick book

Adjective (Base Form)	Modifier Form
많다	인기가 [ ] 가수 – a popular singer
맛있다	[ ] 음식 – delicious food
맛없다	[ ] 음식 – bad/not delicious food
멋지다	[ ] 풍경 – a wonderful view
멀다	[ ] 거리 – a far/long distance
무겁다	[ ] 상자 – a heavy box
무섭다	[ ] 영화 – a horror movie
미안하다	[ ] 마음 – a sorry heart
바쁘다	[ ] 하루 – a busy day
반갑다	[ ] 친구 – a friend you're glad to meet
밝다	[ ] 빛 – a bright light
배고프다	[ ] 호랑이 – a hungry tiger
부드럽다	[ ] 이불 – a soft blanket
부지런하다	[ ] 직원 – a diligent employee
불편하다	[ ] 자세 – an uncomfortable posture
비싸다	[ ] 가방 – an expensive bag
시원하다	[ ] 날씨 – cool weather
시끄럽다	[ ] 교실 – a noisy classroom

Adjective (Base Form)	Modifier Form
싸다	[ ] 물건 – a cheap item
슬프다	[ ] 영화 – a sad movie
쉽다	[ ] 단어 – an easy word
쓰다	[ ] 커피 – bitter coffee
아름답다	[ ] 여자 – a beautiful woman
아프다	[ ] 환자 – a sick patient
어둡다	[ ] 밤 – dark night
어렵다	[ ] 시험 – a difficult exam
어리다	[ ] 아이 – a young kid
예쁘다	[ ] 꽃 – pretty flower
이상하다	[ ] 습관 – a strange/weird habit
외롭다	[ ] 남자 – a lonely man
유명하다	[ ] 연예인 – a famous celebrity
작다	[ ] 집 – a small house
재미있다	[ ] 책 – a fun book
재미없다	[ ] 책 – a boring book
조용하다	[ ] 방 – a quiet room
좁다	[ ] 길 – a narrow road

Adjective (Base Form)	Modifier Form
좋다	[ ] 성격 – a good personality
중요하다	[ ] 조언 – important advice
즐겁다	[ ] 시간 – an enjoyable time
짧다	[ ] 머리 – short hair
지루하다	[ ] 책 – a boring book
차갑다	[ ] 물 – cold water
착하다	[ ] 사람 – a good-hearted person
춥다	[ ] 날씨 – cold weather
친절하다	[ ] 직원 – a kind employee
편하다	[ ] 의자 – a comfortable chair
피곤하다	[ ] 하루 – a tiring day
행복하다	[ ] 가족 – a happy family
흐리다	[ ] 날씨 – cloudy weather
흔하다	[ ] 이름 – a common name
힘들다	[ ] 일 – a hard task

8 For each underlined part, decide whether it is the modifier form or the predicate form of the adjective, and then write the translation of the sentence.

① 건강한 음식을 먹었어요.
(modifier / predicate)

→ ______

채소는 건강해요.
(modifier / predicate)

→ ______

② 여름에는 날씨가 더워요.
(modifier / predicate)

→ ______

더운 날씨를 싫어해요.
(modifier / predicate)

→ ______

③ 짧은 머리를 좋아해요.
(modifier / predicate)

→ ______

저는 머리가 짧아요.
(modifier / predicate)

→ ______

④ 오늘은 바쁜 하루였어요.
(modifier / predicate)

→ ______

엄마는 항상 바빠요.
(modifier / predicate)

→

⑤ 배고픈 고양이에게 밥을 줬어요.
(modifier / predicate)

→

너무 배고파요.
(modifier / predicate)

→

⑥ 의자가 불편해요.
(modifier / predicate)

→

불편한 의자에 앉았어요.
(modifier / predicate)

→

⑦ 예쁜 신발을 샀어요.
(modifier / predicate)

→

신발이 예뻐요.
(modifier / predicate)

→

⑧ 이상한 사람을 만났어요.
(modifier / predicate)

→ ______________________________

그 사람 좀 이상해요.
(modifier / predicate)

→ ______________________________

9 Listen to the audio and write the adjective you hear in the blank. Then, write the meaning of the full sentence in English (or in your preferred language).

TRACK 03

① [ ] 사진을 찍었어요.

→ ______________________________

② 남자친구가 저에게 [ ] 꽃을 줬어요.

→ ______________________________

③ 지수는 [ ] 친구예요.

→ ______________________________

④ [ ] 가수를 봤어요.

→ ______________________________

⑤ [ ] 지갑을 샀어요.

→ ______________________________

10 Fill in the blank with the correct modifier form of the adjective.

① 저는 [   ] 영화를 안 봐요.

I don't watch scary movies.

② 오늘은 [   ] 하루였어요.

Today was a long day.

③ [   ] 음식을 좋아해요.

I like sweet food.

④ 저녁으로 [   ] 스테이크를 먹었어요.

I had a delicious steak for dinner.

⑤ [   ] 책을 읽었어요.

I read an interesting book.

3 Negating Verbs and Adjectives

1 Turn the following sentences into their negative forms using both 안 and -지 않다. After that, write the English meaning for each negative sentence.

Present Tense

e.g. 저는 커피를 마셔요. (마시다: to drink)

↔ 안: 저는 커피를 안 + 마셔요.
not + drink (present tense conjugation)

-지 않다: 저는 커피를 마시지 않아요.
Stem + 지 않다's present tense conjugation

→ I don't drink coffee.

① **저는 아침을 먹어요.** (먹다: to eat)

↔ 안:

-지 않다:

→

② **제 친구들은 고양이를 좋아해요.** (좋아하다: to like)

↔ 안:

-지 않다:

→

③ **혼자 살아요.** (살다: to live)

↔ 안:

-지 않다:

→

④ **주말에 일해요.** (일하다: to work)

↔ 안:

-지 않다:

→

Past Tense

e.g. 커피를 마셨어요. (마시다: to drink)

↔ 안: 저는 커피를 안 + 마셨어요.

not + drank (past tense conjugation)

-지 않다: 저는 커피를 마시지 않았어요.

Stem + 지 않다's past tense conjugation

→ I didn't drink coffee.

⑤ 그 영화를 봤어요. (보다: to watch)

↔ 안:

-지 않다:

→

⑥ 친구를 기다렸어요. (기다리다: to wait)

↔ 안:

-지 않다:

→

⑦ 어제 날씨가 따뜻했어요. (따뜻하다: to be warm)

↔ 안:

-지 않다:

→

⑧ 여자친구한테 선물을 줬어요. (주다: to give)

↔ 안:

-지 않다:

→

Future Tense

e.g. 커피를 마실 거예요. (마시다: to drink)

↔ 안: 저는 커피를 안 + 마실 거예요.

not + will drink (future tense conjugation)

-지 않다: 저는 커피를 마시지 않을 거예요.

Stem + 지 않다's future tense conjugation

→ I won't drink coffee.

⑨ 시험이 어려울 거예요. (어렵다: to be difficult)

↔ 안:

-지 않다:

→

⑩ 아빠가 내일 바쁠 거예요. (바쁘다: to be busy)

↔ 안:

-지 않다:

→

⑪ 집에서 공부할 거예요. (공부하다: to study)

↔ 안:

-지 않다:

→

⑫ 양말을 신을 거예요. (신다: to wear (footwear))

↔ 안:

-지 않다:

→

Little Checkpoint Read & Tick ☑

1 **안** is placed directly before the verb or adjective's conjugation that you want to negate. ☐

2 -**지 않다** attaches to the stem of a verb or adjective and is conjugated into present, past, or future tense. ☐

3 When using **안** with verbs that end in -**하다** (such as **공부하다** or **운동하다**), you need to separate the noun part from **하다** and place **안** in between. ☐

☒ Incorrect: **안 공부하다, 안 운동하다**

☑ Correct: **공부 안 하다, 운동 안 하다**
(You can also put the object marker. **공부를 안 하다, 운동을 안 하다**)

4 However, some -**하다** verbs like **좋아하다** and **정하다** are not **noun + 하다** combinations. Therefore, you cannot split them. ☐

☒ Incorrect: **좋아 안 하다, 정 안 하다**

☑ Correct: **안 좋아하다, 안 정하다**

5 For adjectives ending in -**하다** (e.g., **친절하다, 건강하다**), do not split the word. Just place **안** directly before the adjective. ☐

☒ Incorrect: **친절 안 하다, 건강 안 하다**

☑ Correct: **안 친절하다, 안 건강하다**

2 Turn the following sentences into their negative forms using the opposite word. After that, write the English meaning for each negative sentence.

① 이 사람은 제 친구예요.

↔ 이 사람은 제 친구가 [   ].

→ ______________________________

② 고양이가 방에 있어요.

↔ 고양이가 방에 [   ].

→ ______________________________

③ 저는 그 단어를 알아요.

↔ 저는 그 단어를 [   ].

→ ______________________________

④ 저는 한국어를 잘해요.

↔ 저는 한국어를 [   ].

→ ______________________________

Little Checkpoint **Read & Tick**

1 When negating verbs like **이다** (to be), **있다** (to exist/have), **알다** (to know), and **잘하다** (to do well, to be good) it's much more natural to use their opposite forms **아니다** (to not be), **없다** (to not exist/not have), **모르다** (to not know), and **못하다** (to not do well), than to use 안 or -지 않다. ☐

2 Note that **모르다** is an irregular verb that follows the **르** irregular conjugation rule. ☐

3 Translate the following into Korean using the -요 ending.

① The bag is too expensive. I won't buy it. (Use 안. / 사다: to buy)

→

② I didn't call Mom today. (Use 안. / 전화하다: to call)

→

③ The airport is not far from here. (Use -지 않다. / ~에서 멀다: to be far from~)

→

④ I wasn't tired yesterday. (Use 안. / 피곤하다: to be tired)

→

⑤ The teacher doesn't know my name.

→

⑥ I won't tell. (Use -지 않다. / 말하다: tell)

→

4 The -ㅂ/습니다 Ending

Like the -요 ending, the -ㅂ/습니다 ending is also a 존댓말 form, but it sounds more formal.

Different rules apply when conjugating these two endings in different tenses.

Present Tense

If a verb or adjective's stem ends with a vowel, you attach -ㅂ니다 to the stem.

e.g. 마시다 → 마십니다

좋아하다 → 좋아합니다

If the stem ends with a consonant, you attach -습니다.

e.g. 있다 → 있습니다

어렵다 → 어렵습니다

Past Tense

To form the past tense in the -ㅂ/습니다 style, take the present tense conjugated form of a verb or adjective and add -ㅆ습니다.

e.g. 마시다 → 마셔 (present conjugation) + ㅆ습니다 → 마셨습니다

좋아하다 → 좋아해 + ㅆ습니다 → 좋아했습니다

있다 → 있어 + ㅆ습니다 → 있었습니다

어렵다 → 어려워 + ㅆ습니다 → 어려웠습니다

Future Tense

Similar to the -요 ending, you attach -ㄹ/을 거 to the stem. Then, you add ㅂ니다.

e.g. 마시다 → 마시 + ㄹ 거 + ㅂ니다 → 마실 겁니다

좋아하다 → 좋아하 +ㄹ 거 + ㅂ니다 → 좋아할 겁니다

있다 → 있 + 을 거 + ㅂ니다 → 있을 겁니다

어렵다 → 어렵 + 을 거 + ㅂ니다 → 어려울* 겁니다

(*the ㅂ irregular)

You may also see -ㄹ/을 것입니다 used instead of -ㄹ/을 겁니다. Both are the correct future forms of the -ㅂ/습니다 enidng. In this book, however, we will practice with -ㄹ/을 겁니다.

Little Checkpoint Read & Tick ☑

Things to Note for Each Tense of -ㅂ/습니다

1. Present Tense

Verbs and adjectives ending in ㄹ behave irregularly: the final ㄹ is dropped before attaching -ㅂ니다. ☐

e.g. 살다 → 삽니다, 달다 → 답니다

Other than this, no irregular rules apply to the present tense form of -ㅂ/습니다.

For example, verbs/adjectives like 듣다 (ㄷ-irregular), 덥다 (ㅂ-irregular), or 쓰다 (ㅡ-irregular) normally follow their respective irregular rules in other conjugations. However, with -ㅂ/습니다, you simply attach either -ㅂ니다 or -습니다 to the stem without any changes. ☐

e.g. 듣습니다, 덥습니다, 씁니다

2. Past Tense

To form the past tense, first conjugate the verb/adjective into its present tense form, and then add -ㅆ습니다. At this stage, all irregular conjugation rules apply when forming the present tense base. ☐

e.g. 듣다 → 들어 → 들었습니다, 덥다 → 더워 → 더웠습니다

3. Future Tense

Likewise, the same applies to the future: when you attach -ㄹ/을 to the stem, any relevant irregular rules apply. For example, 덥다 + -ㄹ/을 becomes 더울, and 듣다 + -ㄹ/을 becomes 들을. This rule is the same whether you use the -거예요 ending or the -겁니다 ending. ☐

e.g. 덥다 → 더울 거예요 / 더울 겁니다,
듣다 → 들을 거예요 / 들을 겁니다

1 Let's practice conjugating the following adjectives and verbs with the -ㅂ/습니다 ending.

Verb/Adjective (Base Form)	Present Tense	Past Tense	Future Tense
가다 to go			
가르치다 to teach			
고맙다 to be thankful			
공부하다 to study			
기쁘다 to be happy, to be glad			
기다리다 to wait			
괜찮다 to be okay			
깨끗하다 to be clean			
놀다 to play, to hang out			
닫다 to close			
덥다 to be hot [weather]			
도와주다 to help			
되다 to become			
듣다 to listen			
만나다 to meet			
많다 to be many			
먹다 to eat			
바쁘다 to be busy			
반갑다 to be glad (to meet sb)			
배우다 to learn			
보내다 to send			

Verb/Adjective (Base Form)	Present Tense	Past Tense	Future Tense
보다 to see, to look			
사다 to buy			
살다 to live			
슬프다 to be sad			
쓰다 ① to use, ② to write, ③ to be bitter			
아니다 to be not			
알다 to know			
없다 to be not there, to not have			
웃다 to laugh, to smile			
이다 to be			
있다 to be there, to have			
자다 to sleep			
작다 to be small			
잘하다 to be good at			
좋다 to be good			
좋아하다 to like			
크다 to be big			
행복하다 to be happy			
힘들다 to be challenging, to be difficult			
-지 않다 negation form			

2 Change the following -요 ending sentences to the -ㅂ/습니다 form, and write the translation in English.

① 저는 한국 사람이 아니에요.

-ㅂ/습니다

→

② 저희 부모님은 한국에 살아요.

→

③ 요즘 한국어를 배워요. 조금 어려워요.

→

④ 저는 형제가 없어요. 외동이에요. (외동: only child)

→

⑤ 피곤해요. 일찍 잘 거예요.

→

⑥ 매운 음식을 먹지 않아요.

→

⑦ 저는 매일 커피를 마셔요.

→

⑧ 교수님께 메일을 아직 안 보냈어요.

→

⑨ 저는 일요일하고 목요일에 한국어 수업을 들어요.

→

⑩ 선생님은 자주 웃어요. 그리고(and) 친절해요.

→

3 Translate the following sentences using the -ㅂ/습니다 ending.

① I go to school from Monday to Friday.

→ ______

② I'm a nurse. I help sick people. (간호사: nurse)

→ ______

③ I don't like hot weather.

→ ______

④ I am tall. My younger brother is short.

→ ______

⑤ I worked hard yesterday. I will rest at home today.

→ 어제는 ______.

오늘은 ______.

PART 2

10-Day
100 Sentence
Making Challenge

Congratulations on finishing this workbook!
축하해요!

You should be proud of yourself for dedicating so much time and effort to studying Korean with this book.

But instead of stopping here, let's take it one step further with a 100-Sentence Challenge.

We can all agree that reading and understanding sentences that are already written is relatively easy. But creating your own sentences is the hardest part—and also the most rewarding!

That's why I created this special section to help you practice more sentence-making.

This 100-Sentence Challenge will not only improve your **sentence-building skills**, but also strengthen your **comprehension skills** and help you **consolidate the grammar and expressions** you've learned so far, locking them firmly into your memory.

How to use this challenge:

① Write each sentence in Korean twice: once using the -요 ending (casual polite), and once using the -ㅂ/습니다 ending (formal polite).

② After you finish writing, compare your sentences with the model answers in the answer key.

③ Then, listen to the audio recordings for each day's sentences. Since you created the sentences yourself, it will be much easier to understand their meaning when you hear them in Korean. This will also boost your listening comprehension.

☆ If you'd like even more listening practice, you can also use this challenge for dictation exercises instead of sentence-making.

Now, let's get started!

Day 1

1 I learn Korean.

-요

-ㅂ/습니다

2 Korean is a bit difficult.

3 Cats sleep a lot.

4 I'm a good person.

5 I'm at the library right now.

6 I have a Korean friend.

7 I often eat Korean food. (often: 자주)

8 I don't watch TV at night. (TV: 티브이)

9 I don't live in Korea.

10 I will hang out with my friends on the weekend.

Day 2

11 I live with my family.

-요

-ㅂ/습니다

12 I had bread and milk for breakfast.

13 I exercise every day at the gym.

14 I go to school on weekdays. (weekdays: 평일)

15 Buses are too slow. Let's go by train.

16 I don't like spicy food.

17 I wrote my name in Korean.

18 I sent the teacher a long email.

19 I don't have an expensive bag. I only have cheap ones.

20 I don't wear socks in summer.

Day 3

21 I'm a little tired. I will sleep soon. (soon: 곧)

-요

-ㅂ/습니다

22 I spent a good time with my family in the evening.

23 I'm not a student.

24 The Korean class was so fun.

25 I slept alone in my room.

26 I usually study at home. (usually: 주로)

27 I got an email from my coworker. (coworker: 동료)

28 Only I didn't know. (as in, I was the only one that didn't know.)

29 I learned Korean from a native teacher.

30 My dad works on the weekends as well. (as in, weekends as well as other days)

Day 4

31 I learned a lot of difficult words today.

-요

-ㅂ/습니다

32 My friend has a cute daughter. (daughter: 딸)

33 Today is my birthday.

34 I wrote this letter with my hand. (= I hand-wrote this letter.)

35 I traveled by bus in Korea.

36 I watched a movie with my boyfriend at the theatre on Friday.

37 There are students and a teacher in the classroom.

38 I waited for my friend at the subway station. (subway station: 지하철역)

39 It will rain every day from July to August.

40 I will finish the assignment by tomorrow.

Day 5

41 There is no trash can in the park.

-요

-ㅂ/습니다

42 I'm good at cooking.

43 My husband is bad at driving.

44 I will go to Korea in May.

45 I listen to Korean music sometimes. (sometimes: 가끔)

46 Let's rest a bit. (= Let's some rest.)

47 My dad works too hard.

48 I live in a small house.

49 I met a lot of kind people in Korea.

50 It snowed a lot yesterday. (to snow: 눈이 오다)

Day 6

51 It will be cold tomorrow.

-요

-ㅂ/습니다

52 This is my book.

53 I studied Korean with this book.

54 Let's watch a good(= fun/interesting) movie together.

55 I don't like bitter coffee. I like sweet coffee.

56 My stomach hurts.

57 My friends were in Korea last year. Now they are in the US.

58 I have a younger sister and a younger brother.

59 I will take a shower with cold water.

60 This movie is too short.

Day 7

61 I hate hot weather.

-요

-ㅂ/습니다

62 These shoes aren't pretty.

63 The airport isn't far from here.

64 I won't watch sad movies today.

65 I was too busy yesterday.

66 It's too expensive. I won't buy it.

67 I made delicious Korean food.

68 I already told my friends.

69 I don't know this word. I will ask the teacher.

70 The guests sat on the couch. (couch: 소파)

Day 8

71 I'm at the company. (= I'm at work.)

-요

-ㅂ/습니다

72 I have a company. / There is a company.

73 I work at a company.

74 The cat is in my room.

75 Jisu will probably know. (probably: 아마)

76 I bought some pretty shoes. I gave them to my friend.

77 I study only at school.

78 I will be in Korea only in March.

79 Mom cooks in the kitchen. (kitchen: 부엌)

80 I raise a cat at home.

Day 9

81 I put some sugar in the coffee.

-요

-ㅂ/습니다

82 I borrowed some clothes from my friend.

83 I don't work on Saturday and Sunday.

84 I don't have friends. I only hang out with my older sister.

85 That house is really big.

86 I don't have cash right now. I will buy it later. (later: 나중에)

87 I read that book last year. It was good.

88 There's a bathroom here.

89 My family is not at home right now.

90 Today was a happy day.

Day 10

91 I speak English and Korean.

-요

-ㅂ/습니다

92 Mom didn't call me today.

93 I heard good news from the teacher.

94 The exam was too easy.

95 The homework won't be too difficult.

96 My mom doesn't eat meat.

97 Let's converse only in Korean.

98 I will wait for the reply until tomorrow. (reply: 답장)

99 I was bitten by a mosquito. It hurts.

100 I teach English to Korean people.

ANSWER

PART 1 Workbook

CHAPTER 1 Particles

은/는 & 이/가

1. ① 은, 는 ② 이, 가
2. ① 는 ② 은 ③ 는 ④ 은 ⑤ 는 ⑥ 은 ⑦ 은 ⑧ 는
3. ① 이 ② 가 ③ 이 ④ 가 ⑤ 이 ⑥ 이 ⑦ 가
4. ① 전 ② 넌 ③ 이건
5. ① 제가 ② 이게 ③ 네가

을/를

1. 을, 를
2. ① 을 ② 을 ③ 를 ④ 을 ⑤ 를 ⑥ 를 ⑦ 를 ⑧ 을
3. ① 가, 를 ② 가 ③ 가, 을 ④ 이 ⑤ 을 ⑥ 이, 을 ⑦ 을 ⑧ 이

의

1. ① 의 ② 의
2. ① 저의 ② 제
3. ① 나의 ② 내
4. ① 너의 ② 네

에 & 에서

1 ① 에 ② 에 ③ 에 ④ 에 ⑤ 에서 ⑥ 에/에서 ⑦ 에서 ⑧ -, 에 ⑨ 에 ⑩ 에,에서

*⑥ Both 에 살다 and 에서 살다 can be used to mean "to live in [somewhere].
⑧ Time adverbs such as 어제 (yesterday), 오늘 (today), and 내일 (tomorrow) do not take the time particle 에 and are used by themselves.

부터, 에서 & 까지

1 ① 부터, 까지 ② 에서, 까지 ③ 까지 ④ 까지 ⑤ 부터 ⑥ 부터 ⑦ 까지

에게(서)/한테(서)

1 ① 에게/한테 → I told my friend.
② 에게/한테 → I will call mom.
③ 에게/한테, 을 → I will give a present to my girlfriend.
④ 에게/한테, 을 → I sent an email to a coworker.

2 ① 에게/에게서, 를
→ I learned Korean from a native teacher.
② 한테/한테서, 를
→ I got an apology from a friend.
③ 한테/한테서, 을
→ I heard good news from Mom.
④ 에게/에게서, 을
→ I borrowed a book from my younger sister.
⑤ 에게, 를
→ Miss Vicky teaches Korean to foreigners.
⑥ 을
→ I teach children.
When a sentence shows both what is being taught and who is being taught, the person is marked with -에게/-한테. But if the sentence only mentions who is being taught (and not what), then that person is marked with the object marker 을/를.

⑦ 에

→ Did you water the flower?

께 vs. 께서

1 ① 께 ② 께서 ③ 께 ④ 께서

와/과, (이)랑 & 하고

1 ① with → I went to the department store with Mom.

② and → I bought strawberries and kiwis.

③ and → I have a daughter and a son.

④ and → I like spring and winter.

⑤ with → I hung out with my friend.

⑥ and, with → Today, I went to the market with my dad and grandma.

2 ③ **아이들랑** → **아이들이랑** (For **(이)랑**, you use **랑** if the preceding noun ends in a vowel, and **이랑** if the preceding noun ends in a consonant.)

① I raise a dog and a cat.

② I bought a pen and a pencil at the store.

③ I had dinner with children.

④ I went traveling with my family.

⑤ Let's learn Korean together (with me).

(으)로

1 ① 으로 → I had bread and coffee for breakfast.

② 으로 → Go right. / Turn right.

③ 로 → I talked with the teacher in Korean.

④ 로 → I went from Seoul Station to Ilsan by subway.
(으)로 Irregular: When (으)로 is attached to a noun ending in the final consonants ㄹ, you should use 로, not 으로.

⑤ 로 → I drank coke with a straw.

⑥ 로 → Which one will you choose? / What will you choose?

도 & 만

1 ① ⓐ도 (I like dramas. I also like movies.)
② ⓑ만 (I don't have any cash. I only have a card.)
③ ⓐ도 (I'm a doctor. My husband is also a doctor.)
④ ⓑ만 (My friends aren't good at Korean. I'm the only one who is.)

2 ① ⓓ (I study only in the library.)
② ⓒ (This store exists only in Seoul.)
③ ⓐ (This summer, I'll go to Korea. I will also go to Japan.)
④ ⓐ, ⓑ (These days, I talk only in (only using) Korean.)
⑤ ⓑ (I studied Korean using books. I also studied using videos.)
⑥ ⓐ, ⓒ (I only told my secret to Minji.)
⑦ ⓑ (I only took the photo with Sujin.)

3 ① 도 ② 도 ③ 만 or 만을 (The particle 도 can never be paired with topic, subject, or object markers.)

CHAPTER 2 Verbs & Adjectives

1 Verbs

1 (1) Present Tense: 아, 어, stem, ㅘ, ㅝ, ㅕ, 해
(2) Past Tense : ㅆ, 어
(3) Future Tense : ㄹ, 을

2 A, B, C, D, E (all of them)

3

동사 Verb	현재 시제 Present Tense	과거 시제 Past Tense	미래 시제 Future Tense
가다	가(요)	갔어(요)	갈 거야/거예요
가르치다	가르쳐(요)	가르쳤어(요)	가르칠 거야/거예요
공부하다	공부해(요)	공부했어(요)	공부할 거야/거예요

동사 Verb	현재 시제 Present Tense	과거 시제 Past Tense	미래 시제 Future Tense
기다리다	기다려(요)	기다렸어(요)	기다릴 거야/거예요
끝내다	끝내(요)	끝냈어(요)	끝낼 거야/거예요
넣다	넣어(요)	넣었어(요)	넣을 거야/거예요
놀다	놀아(요)	놀았어(요)	놀 거야/거예요
놓다	놓아(요)	놓았어(요)	놓을 거야/거예요
내리다	내려(요)	내렸어(요)	내릴 거야/거예요
닫다	닫아(요)	닫았어(요)	닫을 거야/거예요
도착하다	도착해(요)	도착했어(요)	도착할 거야/거예요
되다	돼(요), 되어(요)	됐어(요), 되었어(요)	될 거야/거예요
듣다	들어(요)	들었어(요)	들을 거야/거예요
마시다	마셔(요)	마셨어(요)	마실 거야/거예요
만나다	만나(요)	만났어(요)	만날 거야/거예요
만들다	만들어(요)	만들었어(요)	만들 거야/거예요
말하다	말해(요)	말했어(요)	말할 거야/거예요
먹다	먹어(요)	먹었어(요)	먹을 거야/거예요
물어보다	물어봐(요)	물어봤어(요)	물어볼 거야/거예요
받다	받아(요)	받았어(요)	받을 거야/거예요
배우다	배워(요)	배웠어(요)	배울 거야/거예요
벗다	벗어(요)	벗었어(요)	벗을 거야/거예요
보내다	보내(요)	보냈어(요)	보낼 거야/거예요
보다	봐(요)	봤어(요)	볼 거야/거예요

동사 Verb	현재 시제 Present Tense	과거 시제 Past Tense	미래 시제 Future Tense
빌리다	빌려(요)	빌렸어(요)	빌릴 거야/거예요
사다	사(요)	샀어(요)	살 거야/거예요
사랑하다	사랑해(요)	사랑했어(요)	사랑할 거야/거예요
살다	살아(요)	살았어(요)	살 거야/거예요
생각하다	생각해(요)	생각했어(요)	생각할 거야/거예요
서다	서(요)	섰어(요)	설 거야/거예요
쉬다	쉬어(요)	쉬었어(요)	쉴 거야/거예요
시작하다	시작해(요)	시작했어(요)	시작할 거야/거예요
신다	신어(요)	신었어(요)	신을 거야/거예요
싫어하다	싫어해(요)	싫어했어(요)	싫어할 거야/거예요
싸우다	싸워(요)	싸웠어(요)	싸울 거야/거예요
쓰다	써(요)	썼어(요)	쓸 거야/거예요
씻다	씻어(요)	씻었어(요)	씻을 거야/거예요
앉다	앉아(요)	앉았어(요)	앉을 거야/거예요
알다	알아(요)	알았어(요)	알 거야/거예요
없다	없어(요)	없었어(요)	없을 거야/거예요
열다	열어(요)	열었어(요)	열 거야/거예요
오다	와(요)	왔어(요)	올 거야/거예요
외우다	외워(요)	외웠어(요)	외울 거야/거예요
요리하다	요리해(요)	요리했어(요)	요리할 거야/거예요
운동하다	운동해(요)	운동했어(요)	운동할 거야/거예요
운전하다	운전해(요)	운전했어(요)	운전할 거야/거예요

동사 **Verb**	현재 시제 **Present Tense**	과거 시제 **Past Tense**	미래 시제 **Future Tense**
울다	울어(요)	울었어(요)	울 거야/거예요
웃다	웃어(요)	웃었어(요)	웃을 거야/거예요
이야기하다	이야기해(요)	이야기했어(요)	이야기할 거야/거예요
일어나다	일어나(요)	일어났어(요)	일어날 거야/거예요
일하다	일해(요)	일했어(요)	일할 거야/거예요
읽다	읽어(요)	읽었어(요)	읽을 거야/거예요
입다	입어(요)	입었어(요)	입을 거야/거예요
있다	있어(요)	있었어(요)	있을 거야/거예요
자다	자(요)	잤어(요)	잘 거야/거예요
잘하다	잘해(요)	잘했어(요)	잘할 거야/거예요
전화하다	전화해(요)	전화했어(요)	전화할 거야/거예요
좋아하다	좋아해(요)	좋아했어(요)	좋아할 거야/거예요
주다	줘(요)	줬어(요)	줄 거야/거예요
지내다	지내(요)	지냈어(요)	지낼 거야/거예요
(사진을) 찍다	찍어(요)	찍었어(요)	찍을 거야/거예요
청소하다	청소해(요)	청소했어(요)	청소할 거야/거예요
출발하다	출발해(요)	출발했어(요)	출발할 거야/거예요
춤을 추다	춤을 춰(요)	춤을 췄어(요)	춤을 출 거야/거예요
켜다	켜(요)	켰어(요)	켤 거야/거예요
키우다	키워(요)	키웠어(요)	키울 거야/거예요
타다	타(요)	탔어(요)	탈 거야/거예요
하다	해(요)	했어(요)	할 거야/거예요

4

		존댓말	반말
Noun이다 (to be Noun)	When a noun ends in a vowel	예요	야
	When a noun ends in a consonant	이에요	이야
Noun이/가 아니다		아니에요	아니야

5 ① 알아요 ② 만났어요 ③ 봤어요 ④ 먹어요 ⑤ 잘 거예요 ⑥ 쉬어요 ⑦ 공부해요 ⑧ 웃을 거예요 ⑨ 보냈어요, 받았어요 ⑩ 일해요 ⑪ 왔어요 ⑫ 가르쳐요 ⑬ 알 거예요 ⑭ 마셔요 ⑮ 줬어요 ⑯ 만들 거예요, 좋아할 거예요

6 ① 살아 → My parents live in Seoul.

② 닫아 → Close the window. / I close the window.

③ 앉아 → Sit here. / I sit here.

④ 먹었어 → Did you have dinner?

⑤ 갈 거예 → I will go to the gym.

⑥ 가르쳐 → I teach English to students. / I teach students English.

⑦ 빌렸어 → I borrowed the book in the library. / I borrowed the book from the library.

⑧ 공부할 거야 → I will study Korean at home in the evening.

⑨ 일해 → I work in the company/office.

⑩ 받았어 → I received a birthday present from a friend.

⑪ 찍었어 → I took a lot of photos in Korea.

⑫ 내려 → Get off at the next station. / I get off at the next station.

⑬ 일어날 거예 → I will wake up early in the morning tomorrow.

⑭ 이에, 이야 → My friend is Korean.

⑮ 아니에, 아니야 → I'm not Korean.

⑯ 쉬었어 → I took a rest at home on the weekend.

⑰ 좋아해 → My family likes traveling.

7 ① 이에요 ② 이 있어요 ③ 에 있어요 ④ 예요 ⑤ 가 있어요 ⑥ 에 있어요

8 ① 이건 건물이 아니에요.
② 건물이 없어요.
③ 건물에 없어요.
④ 이 사람은 저희 언니가 아니에요.
⑤ 저는 언니가 없어요.
⑥ 언니가 집에 없어요.

9 ① 이 ② 에, 가 ③ 가 ④ 가 ⑤ 를 ⑥ 을 ⑦ 에 ⑧ 에, 에

2 Adjectives

1 워, 울

2 ㅓ, ㅏ, ㅓ

3

형용사 Adjective	현재 시제 Present Tense	과거 시제 Past Tense	미래 시제 Future Tense
가깝다	가까워(요)	가까웠어(요)	가까울 거야/거예요
가볍다	가벼워(요)	가벼웠어(요)	가벼울 거야/거예요
간단하다	간단해(요)	간단했어(요)	간단할 거야/거예요
같다 / 똑같다	같아(요) / 똑같아(요)	같았어(요) / 똑같았어(요)	같을 거야/거예요 똑같을 거야/거예요
건강하다	건강해(요)	건강했어(요)	건강할 거야/거예요
고맙다	고마워(요)	고마웠어(요)	고마울 거야/거예요
괜찮다	괜찮아(요)	괜찮았어(요)	괜찮을 거야/거예요
귀엽다	귀여워(요)	귀여웠어(요)	귀여울 거야/거예요
기쁘다	기뻐(요)	기뻤어(요)	기쁠 거야/거예요
길다	길어(요)	길었어(요)	길 거야/거예요

형용사 **Adjective**	현재 시제 **Present Tense**	과거 시제 **Past Tense**	미래 시제 **Future Tense**
나쁘다	나빠(요)	나빴어(요)	나쁠 거야/거예요
낮다	낮아(요)	낮았어(요)	낮을 거야/거예요
넓다	넓어(요)	넓었어(요)	넓을 거야/거예요
느리다	느려(요)	느렸어(요)	느릴 거야/거예요
늦다	늦어(요)	늦었어(요)	늦을 거야/거예요
달다	달아(요)	달았어(요)	달 거야/거예요
덥다	더워(요)	더웠어(요)	더울 거야/거예요
두껍다	두꺼워(요)	두꺼웠어(요)	두꺼울 거야/거예요
많다	많아(요)	많았어(요)	많을 거야/거예요
맛있다	맛있어(요)	맛있었어(요)	맛있을 거야/거예요
맛없다	맛없어(요)	맛없었어(요)	맛없을 거야/거예요
멋지다	멋져(요)	멋졌어(요)	멋질 거야/거예요
멀다	멀어(요)	멀었어(요)	멀 거야/거예요
무겁다	무거워(요)	무거웠어(요)	무거울 거야/거예요
무섭다	무서워(요)	무서웠어(요)	무서울 거야/거예요
미안하다	미안해(요)	미안했어(요)	미안할 거야/거예요
바쁘다	바빠(요)	바빴어(요)	바쁠 거야/거예요
반갑다	반가워(요)	반가웠어(요)	반가울 거야/거예요
밝다	밝아(요)	밝았어(요)	밝을 거야/거예요
배고프다	배고파(요)	배고팠어(요)	배고플 거야/거예요
부드럽다	부드러워(요)	부드러웠어(요)	부드러울 거야/거예요

형용사 Adjective	현재 시제 **Present Tense**	과거 시제 **Past Tense**	미래 시제 **Future Tense**
부지런하다	부지런해(요)	부지런했어(요)	부지런할 거야/거예요
불편하다	불편해(요)	불편했어(요)	불편할 거야/거예요
비싸다	비싸(요)	비쌌어(요)	비쌀 거야/거예요
시원하다	시원해(요)	시원했어(요)	시원할 거야/거예요
시끄럽다	시끄러워(요)	시끄러웠어(요)	시끄러울 거야/거예요
싸다	싸(요)	쌌어(요)	쌀 거야/거예요
슬프다	슬퍼(요)	슬펐어(요)	슬플 거야/거예요
쉽다	쉬워(요)	쉬웠어(요)	쉬울 거야/거예요
쓰다	써(요)	썼어(요)	쓸 거야/거예요
아름답다	아름다워(요)	아름다웠어(요)	아름다울 거야/거예요
아프다	아파(요)	아팠어(요)	아플 거야/거예요
어둡다	어두워(요)	어두웠어(요)	어두울 거야/거예요
어렵다	어려워(요)	어려웠어(요)	어려울 거야/거예요
어리다	어려(요)	어렸어(요)	어릴 거야/거예요
예쁘다	예뻐(요)	예뻤어(요)	예쁠 거야/거예요
이상하다	이상해(요)	이상했어(요)	이상할 거야/거예요
외롭다	외로워(요)	외로웠어(요)	외로울 거야/거예요
유명하다	유명해(요)	유명했어(요)	유명할 거야/거예요
작다 키가 작다	작아(요)	작았어(요)	작을 거야/거예요
재미있다	재미있어(요)	재미있었어(요)	재미있을 거야/거예요
재미없다	재미없어(요)	재미없었어(요)	재미없을 거야/거예요

3

형용사 Adjective	현재 시제 Present Tense	과거 시제 Past Tense	미래 시제 Future Tense
조용하다	조용해(요)	조용했어(요)	조용할 거야/거예요
좁다	좁아(요)	좁았어(요)	좁을 거야/거예요
좋다	좋아(요)	좋았어(요)	좋을 거야/거예요
중요하다	중요해(요)	중요했어(요)	중요할 거야/거예요
즐겁다	즐거워(요)	즐거웠어(요)	즐거울 거야/거예요
짧다	짧아(요)	짧았어(요)	짧을 거야/거예요
지루하다	지루해(요)	지루했어(요)	지루할 거야/거예요
차갑다	차가워(요)	차가웠어(요)	차가울 거야/거예요
착하다	착해(요)	착했어(요)	착할 거야/거예요
춥다	추워(요)	추웠어(요)	추울 거야/거예요
친절하다	친절해(요)	친절했어(요)	친절할 거야/거예요
크다 키가 크다	커(요)	컸어(요)	클 거야/거예요
편하다	편해(요)	편했어(요)	편할 거야/거예요
피곤하다	피곤해(요)	피곤했어(요)	피곤할 거야/거예요
행복하다	행복해(요)	행복했어(요)	행복할 거야/거예요
흐리다	흐려(요)	흐렸어(요)	흐릴 거야/거예요
흔하다	흔해(요)	흔했어(요)	흔할 거야/거예요
힘들다	힘들어(요)	힘들었어(요)	힘들 거야/거예요

4 ① 좋아요, 더워요

② 나빠요

③ 커요

④ 작아요

⑤ 길어요

⑥ 달아요

⑦ 친절해요

⑧ 멀 거예요

⑨ 바빠요

⑩ 쉬웠어요

⑪ 차가울 거예요

⑫ 어려워요, 재미있어요

⑬ 맛있어요, 매워요

⑭ 느려요

⑮ 길어요, 고파요

5 ① 예뻐요, 비싸요 → These shoes are so pretty. But they're a bit expensive.

② 아파요 → My head hurts. (= I have a headache.)

③ 아름다워요 → The view is so beautiful.

④ 많았어요 → There were many people in the airport.

⑤ 귀여워요 → The cat is cute.

⑥ 가까워요 → The library is close to my home.

⑦ 뜨거울 거예요 → The coffee will be a bit hot.

6 Regular: ㄴ, 은

Irregular: ㄴ, 운, 는

7

Adjective (Base Form)	Modifier Form
가깝다	가까운 공원 – a close/nearby park
가볍다	가벼운 점심 – a light lunch
간단하다	간단한 문장 – a simple sentence
같다	같은 이름 – the same name
건강하다	건강한 음식 – healthy food
고맙다	고마운 친구 – a friend I feel thankful for
귀엽다	귀여운 아기 – a cute baby
기쁘다	기쁜 마음 – a happy heart
길다	긴 머리 – long hair
나쁘다	나쁜 사람 – a bad person
낮다	낮은 건물 – a low building
넓다	넓은 방 – a spacious room
느리다	느린 거북이 – a slow turtle
늦다	늦은 시간 – a late time
달다	단 도넛 – a sweet doughnut
덥다	더운 날씨 – hot weather
두껍다	두꺼운 책 – a thick book

많다	인기가 [많은] 가수 – a popular singer
맛있다	[맛있는] 음식 – delicious food
맛없다	[맛없는] 음식 – bad/not delicious food
멋지다	[멋진] 풍경 – a wonderful view
멀다	[먼] 거리 – a far/long distance
무겁다	[무거운] 상자 – a heavy box
무섭다	[무서운] 영화 – a horror movie
미안하다	[미안한] 마음 – a sorry heart
바쁘다	[바쁜] 하루 – a busy day
반갑다	[반가운] 친구 – a friend you're glad to meet
밝다	[밝은] 빛 – a bright light
배고프다	[배고픈] 호랑이 – a hungry tiger
부드럽다	[부드러운] 이불 – a soft blanket
부지런하다	[부지런한] 직원 – a diligent employee
불편하다	[불편한] 자세 – an uncomfortable posture
비싸다	[비싼] 가방 – an expensive bag
시원하다	[시원한] 날씨 – cool weather
시끄럽다	[시끄러운] 교실 – a noisy classroom

싸다	싼 물건 – a cheap item
슬프다	슬픈 영화 – a sad movie
쉽다	쉬운 단어 – an easy word
쓰다	쓴 커피 – bitter coffee
아름답다	아름다운 여자 – a beautiful woman
아프다	아픈 환자 – a sick patient
어둡다	어두운 밤 – dark night
어렵다	어려운 시험 – a difficult exam
어리다	어린 아이 – a young kid
예쁘다	예쁜 꽃 – a pretty flower
이상하다	이상한 습관 – a strange/weird habit
외롭다	외로운 남자 – a lonely man
유명하다	유명한 연예인 – a famous celebrity
작다	작은 집 – a small house
재미있다	재미있는 책 – a fun book
재미없다	재미없는 책 – a boring book
조용하다	조용한 방 – a quiet room
좁다	좁은 길 – a narrow road

좋다	좋은 성격 – a good personality
중요하다	중요한 조언 – important advice
즐겁다	즐거운 시간 – an enjoyable time
짧다	짧은 머리 – short hair
지루하다	지루한 책 – a boring book
차갑다	차가운 물 – cold water
착하다	착한 사람 – a good-hearted person
춥다	추운 날씨 – cold weather
친절하다	친절한 직원 – a kind employee
편하다	편한 의자 – a comfortable chair
피곤하다	피곤한 하루 – a tiring day
행복하다	행복한 가족 – a happy family
흐리다	흐린 날씨 – cloudy weather
흔하다	흔한 이름 – a common name
힘들다	힘든 일 – a hard task

8

① modifier → I ate healthy food.
predicate → Vegetables are healthy.

② predicate → The weather is hot in summer.
modifier → I hate hot weather.

③ modifier → I like short hair.
predicate → My hair is short. / I have short hair.

④ modifier → Today was a busy day.
predicate → Mom is always busy.

⑤ modifier → I fed a hungry cat.
predicate → I'm so hungry.

⑥ predicate → The chair is uncomfortable.
modifier → I sat on an uncomfortable chair.

⑦ modifier → I bought pretty shoes.
predicate → The shoes are pretty.

⑧ modifier → I met a strange person.
predicate → That person is quite strange.

9

① 멋진 → I took a cool photo.
② 예쁜 → My boyfriend gave me pretty flowers.
③ 좋은 → Jisu is a good friend.
④ 유명한 → I saw a famous singer.
⑤ 비싼 → I bought an expensive wallet.

10

① 무서운
② 긴
③ 단
④ 맛있는
⑤ 재미있는

3 Negating Verbs and Adjectives

1

① 저는 아침을 안 먹어요.
저는 아침을 먹지 않아요.
→ I don't eat breakfast.

② 제 친구들은 고양이를 안 좋아해요.
제 친구들은 고양이를 좋아하지 않아요.

→ My friends don't like cats.

③ 혼자 안 살아요.
혼자 살지 않아요.

→ I don't live alone.

④ 주말에 일 안 해요.
주말에 일하지 않아요.

→ I don't work on the weekends.

⑤ 그 영화를 안 봤어요.
그 영화를 보지 않았어요.

→ I didn't watch that movie.

⑥ 친구를 안 기다렸어요.
친구를 기다리지 않았어요.

→ I didn't wait for my friend.

⑦ 어제 날씨가 안 따뜻했어요.
어제 날씨가 따뜻하지 않았어요.

→ The weather wasn't warm yesterday.

⑧ 여자친구한테 선물을 안 줬어요.
여자친구한테 선물을 주지 않았어요.

→ I didn't give a gift to my girlfriend.

⑨ 시험이 안 어려울 거예요.
시험이 어렵지 않을 거예요.

→ The exam won't be difficult.

⑩ 아빠가 내일 안 바쁠 거예요.
아빠가 내일 바쁘지 않을 거예요.

→ Dad won't be busy tomorrow.

⑪ 집에서 공부 안 할 거예요.
집에서 공부하지 않을 거예요.

→ I won't study at home.

⑫ 양말을 안 신을 거예요.
양말을 신지 않을 거예요.

→ I will not wear socks.

2 ① 아니에요 → This person is not my friend.

② 없어요 → The cat isn't in the room.

③ 몰라요 → I don't know that word.

④ 못해요 → I'm not good at Korean. / I don't speak Korean.

3 ① 가방이 너무 비싸요. 안 살 거예요.

② 오늘 엄마한테/엄마에게 전화 안 했어요.

③ 공항이 여기에서/여기서 멀지 않아요.

④ 어제 안 피곤했어요.

⑤ 선생님은/선생님께서 제 이름을 몰라요.

⑥ 말하지 않을 거예요.

4 The -ㅂ/습니다 Ending

1

Verb/Adjective (Base Form)	Present Tense	Past Tense	Future Tense
가다	갑니다	갔습니다	갈 겁니다
가르치다	가르칩니다	가르쳤습니다	가르칠 겁니다
고맙다	고맙습니다	고마웠습니다	고마울 겁니다
공부하다	공부합니다	공부했습니다	공부할 겁니다
기쁘다	기쁩니다	기뻤습니다	기쁠 겁니다
기다리다	기다립니다	기다렸습니다	기다릴 겁니다
괜찮다	괜찮습니다	괜찮았습니다	괜찮을 겁니다
깨끗하다	깨끗합니다	깨끗했습니다	깨끗할 겁니다
놀다	놉니다	놀았습니다	놀 겁니다

1

Verb/Adjective (Base Form)	Present Tense	Past Tense	Future Tense
닫다	닫습니다	닫았습니다	닫을 겁니다
덥다	덥습니다	더웠습니다	더울 겁니다
도와주다	도와줍니다	도와줬습니다	도와줄 겁니다
되다	됩니다	되었습니다 됐습니다	될 겁니다
듣다	듣습니다	들었습니다	들을 겁니다
만나다	만납니다	만났습니다	만날 겁니다
많다	많습니다	많았습니다	많을 겁니다
먹다	먹습니다	먹었습니다	먹을 겁니다
바쁘다	바쁩니다	바빴습니다	바쁠 겁니다
반갑다	반갑습니다	반가웠습니다	반가울 겁니다
배우다	배웁니다	배웠습니다	배울 겁니다
보내다	보냅니다	보냈습니다	보낼 겁니다
보다	봅니다	봤습니다	볼 겁니다
사다	삽니다	샀습니다	살 겁니다
살다	삽니다	살았습니다	살 겁니다
슬프다	슬픕니다	슬펐습니다	슬플 겁니다
쓰다	씁니다	썼습니다	쓸 겁니다
아니다	아닙니다	아니었습니다	아닐 겁니다
알다	압니다	알았습니다	알 겁니다
없다	없습니다	없었습니다	없을 겁니다

1

Verb/Adjective (Base Form)	Present Tense	Past Tense	Future Tense
웃다	웃습니다	웃었습니다	웃을 겁니다
이다	입니다	이었습니다	일 겁니다
있다	있습니다	있었습니다	있을 겁니다
자다	잡니다	잤습니다	잘 겁니다
작다	작습니다	작았습니다	작을 겁니다
잘하다	잘합니다	잘했습니다	잘할 겁니다
좋다	좋습니다	좋았습니다	좋을 겁니다
좋아하다	좋아합니다	좋아했습니다	좋아할 겁니다
크다	큽니다	컸습니다	클 겁니다
행복하다	행복합니다	행복했습니다	행복할 겁니다
힘들다	힘듭니다	힘들었습니다	힘들 겁니다
-지 않다	-지 않습니다	-지 않았습니다	-지 않을 겁니다

2

① 저는 한국 사람이 아닙니다.

→ I'm not Korean.

② 저희 부모님은 한국에 삽니다.

→ My parents live in Korea.

③ 요즘 한국어를 배웁니다. 조금 어렵습니다.

→ I learn Korean these days. It's bit difficult.

④ 저는 형제가 없습니다. 외동입니다.

→ I don't have siblings. I'm an only child.

⑤ 피곤합니다. 일찍 잘 겁니다.

→ I'm tired. I will go to sleep early.

⑥ **매운 음식을 먹지 않습니다.**

→ I don't eat spicy food.

⑦ **저는 매일 커피를 마십니다.**

→ I drink coffee everyday.

⑧ **교수님께 메일을 아직 안 보냈습니다.**

→ I didn't send the professor an email yet.

⑨ **저는 일요일하고 목요일에 한국어 수업을 듣습니다.**

→ I take Korean classes on Sundays and Thursdays.

⑩ **선생님은 자주 웃습니다. 그리고 친절합니다.**

→ The teacher smiles often. And she is kind.

3 ① 저는 월요일부터 금요일까지 학교에 갑니다.

② 저는 간호사입니다. 아픈 사람들을 도와줍니다.

③ 더운 날씨를 좋아하지 않습니다. / 더운 날씨를 안 좋아합니다.

④ 저는 키가 큽니다. 제 남동생은 키가 작습니다.

⑤ 열심히 일했습니다. 집에서 쉴 겁니다.

PART 2 10-Day 100 Sentence Making Challenge

꿀팁!

As I'm sure you've noticed, there are many different ways to express the same sentence in Korean. This can depend on the sentence ending you choose, the particle you use, adverb placement, and more.

For example, the subject might be shown with 은/는 or 이/가, or left out completely. In some cases, 저는 is correct; in another context, 제가 may sound more natural; and when it's already clear that the subject is "I," the subject may be omitted altogether.
This is the challenge of single-sentence translation practice: without context, there is rarely just one correct answer, which is why it's difficult to list every possible version in the answer sheet.

Please keep this in mind as you work on the translation questions.
If you're unsure whether your answer that is different from the answer sheet might also be correct, you're welcome to check with the online translation tool or reach out to me through my social media. (Based on what you've learned so far, I think you can also trust your intuition to judge for yourself whether your answer is correct or not!)

Day 1

1 저는 한국어를 배워요.
저는 한국어를 배웁니다.

2 한국어는 조금 어려워요.
한국어는 조금 어렵습니다.

3 고양이는 많이 자요.
고양이는 많이 잡니다.

4 저는 좋은 사람이에요.
저는 좋은 사람입니다.

5 저는 지금 도서관에 있어요.
저는 지금 도서관에 있습니다.

6 저는 한국인 친구가 있어요.
저는 한국인 친구가 있습니다.

7 저는 한국 음식을 자주 먹어요.
저는 자주 한국 음식을 먹습니다.

8 저는 밤에 티브이를 안 봐요/보지 않아요.
저는 밤에 티브이를 안 봅니다/보지 않습니다.

9 저는 한국에 안 살아요/살지 않아요.
저는 한국에 안 삽니다/살지 않습니다.

10 저는 주말에 친구들과 놀 거예요.
저는 주말에 친구들과 놀 겁니다.

Day 2

11 저는 가족하고/가족이랑 살아요.
저는 가족과 삽니다.

12 저는 아침으로 빵이랑/빵하고 우유를 먹었어요.
저는 아침으로 빵과 우유를 먹었습니다.

13 저는 매일 헬스장에서 운동해요.
저는 매일 헬스장에서 운동합니다.

14 저는 평일에 학교에 가요.
저는 평일에 학교에 갑니다.

15 버스는 너무 느려요. 기차로 가요.
버스는 너무 느립니다. 기차로 갑시다.

*The suggestive form of -ㅂ/습니다 changes to -ㅂ/습시다.

16 저는 매운 음식을 안 좋아해요/좋아하지 않아요.
저는 매운 음식을 안 좋아합니다/좋아하지 않습니다.

17 저는 한국어로 제 이름을 썼어요.
저는 한국어로 제 이름을 썼습니다.

18 저는 선생님께 긴 이메일을 보냈어요.
저는 선생님께 긴 이메일을 보냈습니다.

19 저는 비싼 가방이 없어요. 싼 가방만 있어요.
저는 비싼 가방이 없습니다. 싼 가방만 있습니다.

20 저는 여름에 양말을 안 신어요/신지 않아요.
저는 여름에 양말을 안 신습니다/신지 않습니다.

Day 3

21 저는 조금 피곤해요. 곧 잘 거예요.
저는 조금 피곤합니다. 곧 잘 겁니다.

22 저녁에 가족하고/가족이랑 즐거운 시간을 보냈어요.
저녁에 가족과 즐거운 시간을 보냈습니다.

23 저는 학생이 아니에요.
저는 학생이 아닙니다.

24 한국어 수업이 아주 재미있었어요.
한국어 수업이 아주 재미있었습니다.

25 제 방에서 혼자 잤어요.
제 방에서 혼자 잤습니다.

26 저는 주로 집에서 공부해요.
저는 주로 집에서 공부합니다.

27 동료한테(서) 이메일을 받았어요.
동료한테(서) 이메일을 받았습니다.

28 저만 몰랐어요.
저만 몰랐습니다.

29 저는 원어민 선생님한테(서) 한국어를 배웠어요.
저는 원어민 선생님한테(서) 한국어를 배웠습니다.

30 아빠는 주말에도 일해요.
아빠는 주말에도 일합니다.

Day 4

31 오늘 어려운 단어를 많이 배웠어요.
오늘 어려운 단어를 많이 배웠습니다.

32 제 친구는 귀여운 딸이 있어요.
제 친구는 귀여운 딸이 있습니다.

33 오늘은 제 생일이에요.
오늘은 제 생일입니다.

34 이 편지를 손으로 썼어요.
이 편지를 손으로 썼습니다.

35 저는 한국에서 버스로 여행했어요.
저는 한국에서 버스로 여행했습니다.

36 저는 금요일에 극장에서 남자친구랑/남자친구하고 영화를 봤어요.
저는 금요일에 극장에서 남자친구와 영화를 봤습니다.

37 교실에는 학생들하고/학생들이랑 선생님이 있어요.
교실에는 학생들과 선생님이 있습니다.

38 저는 지하철역에서 친구를 기다렸어요.
저는 지하철역에서 친구를 기다렸습니다.

39 7월부터 8월까지 매일 비가 올 거예요.
7월부터 8월까지 매일 비가 올 겁니다.

40 저는 내일까지 과제를 끝낼 거예요.
저는 내일까지 과제를 끝낼 겁니다.

Day 5

41 공원에 휴지통이 없어요.
공원에 휴지통이 없습니다.

42 저는 요리를 잘해요.
저는 요리를 잘합니다.

43 제 남편은 운전을 못해요.
제 남편은 운전을 못합니다.

44 저는 5월에 한국에 갈 거예요.
저는 5월에 한국에 갈 겁니다.

45 저는 가끔 한국 음악을 들어요.
저는 가끔 한국 음악을 듣습니다.

46 좀 쉬어요.
좀 쉽시다.

47 아빠는 너무 열심히 일해요.
아빠는 너무 열심히 일합니다.

48 저는 작은 집에 살아요.
저는 작은 집에 삽니다.

49 저는 한국에서 친절한 사람들을 많이 만났어요.
저는 한국에서 친절한 사람들을 많이 만났습니다.

50 어제 눈이 많이 왔어요.
어제 눈이 많이 왔습니다.

Day 6

51 내일(은) 추울 거예요.
내일(은) 추울 겁니다.

52 이건 제 책이에요.
이것은 제 책입니다.

53 저는 이 책으로 한국어를 공부했어요.
저는 이 책으로 한국어를 공부했습니다.

54 같이 재미있는 영화를 봐요.
같이 재미있는 영화를 봅시다.

55 저는 쓴 커피를 안 좋아해요/좋아하지 않아요. 단 커피를 좋아해요.
저는 쓴 커피를 안 좋아합니다/좋아하지 않습니다. 단 커피를 좋아합니다.

56 배가 아파요.
배가 아픕니다.

57 제 친구들은 작년에 한국에 있었어요. 지금은 미국에 있어요.
제 친구들은 작년에 한국에 있었습니다. 지금은 미국에 있습니다.

58 저는 여동생과 남동생이 있어요.
저는 여동생과 남동생이 있습니다.

59 저는 찬물로 샤워할 거예요.
저는 찬물로 샤워할 겁니다.

60 이 영화는 너무 짧아요.
이 영화는 너무 짧습니다.

Day 7

61 저는 더운 날씨를 싫어해요.
저는 더운 날씨를 싫어합니다.

62 이 신발은 예쁘지 않아요.
이 신발은 예쁘지 않습니다.

63 공항은 여기에서 멀지 않아요.
공항은 여기에서 멀지 않습니다.

64 오늘(은) 슬픈 영화를 안 볼 거예요/보지 않을 거예요.
오늘(은) 슬픈 영화를 안 볼 겁니다/보지 않을 겁니다.

65 저는 어제 너무 바빴어요.
저는 어제 너무 바빴습니다.

66 너무 비싸요. 안 살 거예요/사지 않을 거예요.
너무 비쌉니다. 안 살 겁니다/사지 않을 겁니다.

67 저는 맛있는 한국 음식을 만들었어요.
저는 맛있는 한국 음식을 만들었습니다.

68 저는 이미 친구들에게 말했어요.
저는 이미 친구들에게 말했습니다.

69 저는 이 단어를 몰라요. 선생님께 물어볼 거예요.
저는 이 단어를 모릅니다. 선생님께 물어볼 겁니다.

70 손님들이 소파에 앉았어요.
손님들이 소파에 앉았습니다.

Day 8

71 저는 회사에 있어요.
저는 회사에 있습니다.

72 회사가 있어요.
회사가 있습니다.

73 저는 회사에서 일해요.
저는 회사에서 일합니다.

74 고양이가 제 방에 있어요.
고양이가 제 방에 있습니다.

75 지수가 아마 알 거예요.
아마 지수가 알 겁니다.

76 저는 예쁜 신발을 샀어요. 친구에게 줬어요.
저는 예쁜 신발을 샀습니다. 친구에게 줬습니다.

77 저는 학교에서만 공부해요.
저는 학교에서만 공부합니다.

78 저는 3월에만 한국에 있을 거예요.
저는 3월에만 한국에 있을 겁니다.

79 엄마가 부엌에서 요리해요.
엄마가 부엌에서 요리합니다.

80 저는 집에서 고양이를 키워요.
저는 집에서 고양이를 키웁니다.

Day 9

81 커피에 설탕을 좀 넣었어요.
커피에 설탕을 좀 넣었습니다.

82 친구에게 옷을 좀 빌렸어요.
친구에게 옷을 좀 빌렸습니다.

83 저는 토요일하고/토요일이랑 일요일에는 일을 안 해요/일을 하지 않아요.
저는 토요일과 일요일에는 일을 안 합니다/하지 않습니다.

84 저는 친구가 없어요. 언니랑만/언니하고만 놀아요.
저는 친구가 없습니다. 언니와만 놉니다.

85 저 집은 정말 커요.
저 집은 정말 큽니다.

86 저는 지금 현금이 없어요. 나중에 살 거예요.
저는 지금 현금이 없습니다. 나중에 살 겁니다.

87 저는 작년에 그 책을 읽었어요. 좋았어요.
저는 작년에 그 책을 읽었습니다. 좋았습니다.

88 여기(에) 화장실이 있어요.
여기(에) 화장실이 있습니다.

89 저희 가족은 지금 집에 없어요.
저희 가족은 지금 집에 없습니다.

90 오늘은 행복한 하루였어요.
오늘은 행복한 하루였습니다.

Day 10

91 저는 영어하고 한국어를 해요.
저는 영어하고 한국어를 합니다.

92 엄마가 오늘 저한테 전화를 안 했어요/하지 않았어요.
엄마가 오늘 저한테 전화를 안 했습니다/하지 않았습니다.

93 저는 선생님께 좋은 소식을 들었어요.
저는 선생님께 좋은 소식을 들었습니다.

94 시험이 너무 쉬웠어요.
시험이 너무 쉬웠습니다.

95 숙제가 너무 어렵지 않을 거예요.
숙제가 너무 어렵지 않을 겁니다.

96 엄마는 고기를 안 먹어요/먹지 않아요.
엄마는 고기를 안 먹습니다/먹지 않습니다.

97 한국어로만 대화해요.
한국어로만 대화합시다.

98 내일까지 답장을 기다릴 거예요.
내일까지 답장을 기다릴 겁니다.

99 모기에 물렸어요. 아파요.
모기에 물렸습니다. 아픕니다.

100 저는 한국 사람들에게 영어를 가르쳐요.
저는 한국인들에게 영어를 가르칩니다.

Vocabulary QR Codes

To help you review the vocabulary in this book, we've prepared the following resources:

200 Korean Words from this Book (Nouns & Adverbs)

This QR code gives you access to a downloadable PDF that lists 200 nouns and adverbs used in this book. If you come across unfamiliar words while working through the workbook, you can of course look them up in a dictionary, but you may find it easier to check this list.

Quizlet Vocabulary Sets (Verbs, Adjectives, and the 200 Nouns and Adverbs)

This QR code takes you to Quizlet sets that include the verbs, adjectives, and the 200 nouns and adverbs from this book.

(Quizlet is a free study website. Without logging in, you can use only the flashcard feature. By creating a free account and logging in, you can access additional study tools and features.)